Muse of Fire

NIGEL KRAUTH

Current Theatre Series
published by Currency Press, Sydney
in association with the State Theatre Company of South Australia

CURRENT THEATRE SERIES

First published in 1985
by Currency Press Pty Ltd,
P.O. Box 452 Paddington,
N.S.W. 2021, Australia,
in association with the State Theatre
Company of South Australia

National Library of Australia card number
and ISBN 0 86819 133 7

Typeset and printed by Bridge Printery,
Sydney

Publication assisted by the Literature Board of the Australia
Council, the Federal Government's arts funding and advisory
body.

Muse of Fire was first performed by the State Theatre
Company of South Australia at the Playhouse, Adelaide
Festival Centre, on 3 August 1985 with the following cast:

GEORGE TRAFFORD	Douglas Hedge
ROSIE BELLOWES	Natalie Bate
MOLLY TRAFFORD	Deborah Kennedy
LOUIS ESSON, PLAYER AVIATOR	Andrew Tighe
ELTON HIGGS	Peter Finlay
MUSIC PLUGGER, PIANIST	Ian Farr
MAYOR, SOLICITOR, REPORTER, SECOND STAGEHAND, SECOND CHEMIST	Ross Williams
PRIVATE INVESTIGATOR, FIRST STAGEHAND, NEWSBOY, PHOTOGRAPHER, FIRST CHEMIST	William Zappa
WORKER, AVIATOR, YOUNG ACTOR, INSURANCE ASSESSOR	Terry Crawford
CONTRACTOR, NEWSPAPER MAGNATE, OLD ACTOR, POLICEMAN	David Kendall
CARETAKER WOMAN, THIRD ACTRESS	Joan Murray
OLD ACTRESS	Dina Panozzo
YOUNG ACTRESS, SEAMSTRESS	Morna Seres

Directed by Keith Gallasch
Designed by Colin Mitchell
Lighting design by John Commeadow
Musical Direction by Ian Farr

CHARACTERS

GEORGE TRAFFORD, an actor-manager and theatre
    owner
ROSIE BELLOWES, an actress, his mistress
MOLLY TRAFFORD, George's estranged wife and former
    leading lady
LOUIS ESSON, a playwright
ELTON HIGGS, the stagehands' union leader
MUSIC PLUGGER
CARETAKER WOMAN
FIRST STAGEHAND
SECOND STAGEHAND
SEAMSTRESS
BUILDING CONTRACTOR
MAYOR
NEWSPAPER MAGNATE
AVIATOR
OLD ACTRESS
YOUNG ACTRESS
THIRD ACTRESS
PLAYER PILOT
YOUNG ACTOR
SOLICITOR
FIRST CHEMIST
SECOND CHEMIST
OLD ACTOR
PRIVATE INVESTIGATOR
INSURANCE ASSESSOR
Building workers, newsboy, piano accompanist,
reporters, photographers

SETTING

The action takes place on the stage of the Empire
Theatre, Pitt Street, Sydney, in 1910. The set comprises a
proscenium arch with the wings on either side exposed.

AUTHOR'S NOTE

The characters and events in this play are entirely
imaginary and bear no relation to any real person or
actual happening.

The text here published is that presented at rehearsals for
the first production. Subsequent revisions are not
included.

ACT ONE

SCENE ONE

Blackout. During the scene lights come up gradually on TRAFFORD, ROSIE *and* MOLLY. TRAFFORD, *dressed in street clothes, wears an aviator's leather cap and goggles. He hangs at the end of a wire in a flying position. Beneath him are* ROSIE *and* MOLLY. *They stand back to back.*

TRAFFORD: [*softly, gradually building to a shout*] . . . this cell . . . this worm . . . this world's end . . . this beginning . . . this drowning . . . this suspension . . . of disbelief . . . this cutting loose . . . this puppet . . . this plaything . . . this passion . . . this ascent . . . this seeing, soaring . . . this flight . . . this tearing . . . this vision!

ROSIE: Ever since I was a little girl I wanted to be an explorer. It's not an acceptable career. These days, wanting any career gets a woman into trouble. But there are those who go forth, who venture. Across deserts, through jungles. Marion North, Beatrice Grimshaw, Elinor Francks. Intrepid women in the world's dark corners. How those names shine for me. But what do they discover, those lone women adventurers in the world's trackless wastes? Not love.

TRAFFORD: [*jerking to life*] The fire inside! Adventure! Heroics! The new century's romance! Internal combustion!

MOLLY: Remember me in *The Convict Maid*? They applauded for hours. Or in *Sweet Sal Of The Southern Cross*? They called me back over and over . . . I lost count how many times. And *The Girl From Sandy Hollow*! They stood on their seats, they poured champagne from the balconies. They smothered me with flowers. They tore the dressing-room door from its hinges, just so they could kiss my hand. Ah! This theatre! [*Blackout. We hear the sound of sledgehammers demolishing a wall.*]

SCENE TWO

Blackout. The sledgehammer continues and we hear a wall falling. The piano begins playing a lively popular tune of 1910. It continues over the sound of the sledgehammer and more wall falling. Then suddenly the lights come on. It is afternoon, on the stage of the Empire Theatre. The MUSIC PLUGGER *is at the piano.* TRAFFORD *works at his desk, tossing papers around. The sledgehammer begins again.*

MUSIC PLUGGER: What do you think of this one, Mr Trafford?

TRAFFORD: [*not listening*] I'm listening. [*She stops playing and selects a new sheet of music.*]

MUSIC PLUGGER: I don't think you like it.

TRAFFORD: It's bright. It might be useful.

MUSIC PLUGGER: It took New York by storm. [*She starts playing a new tune.* TRAFFORD *goes to the wings.*]

TRAFFORD: [*shouting*] Ethel! [*The* CARETAKER WOMAN *enters carrying a bird in a cage.*]

CARETAKER WOMAN: Poor little fellow.
All the noise

[TRAFFORD *comes back to his desk.
He sees the* CARETAKER WOMAN.]

TRAFFORD: What's this?

CARETAKER WOMAN: He doesn't like the
noise.

[*The sound of the sledgehammer
begins again.*]

CARETAKER WOMAN: See? He's upset.

TRAFFORD: [*at his papers*] He's not
upset. He's safe in there.

CARETAKER WOMAN: He wants to go
outside.

[*She exits.*]

TRAFFORD: [*checking his fob watch and
shouting again*] Ethel! Where is that
woman?

[*Pause. He listens to the piano music
briefly.*]

I wonder what the statistics on
theatre manager suicides are?

MUSIC PLUGGER: Does this take your
fancy?

[*She continues playing over the sound
of the sledgehammer, wall falling and
the sound of rubble being shovelled
into a barrow.*]

TRAFFORD: 'Sounds and sweet airs, that
give delight and hurt not'. Dear God
in heaven.

[*The* SEAMSTRESS *enters in a rush,
carrying a king's robe. She has pins in
her mouth.*]

SEAMSTRESS: Sorry, Mr Trafford.

[TRAFFORD *spreads out his arms. The*
SEAMSTRESS *turns him round and puts
the robe on him. Two* STAGEHANDS
*carry on a throne and place it centre-
stage. A backcloth depicting blue sky
with clouds begins a slow descent.*]

TRAFFORD: 'This chaos, when degree is
suffocate, follows the choking'.

SEAMSTRESS: Don't think I know that
one, sir.

TRAFFORD: Ulysses to Agamemnon.
They are contemplating the sacking
of Troy. Don't you remember?

SEAMSTRESS: [*kneeling to pin up the
hem*] I'm just wardrobe, sir.
Shakespeare goes over my head. Arms
up, please, sir.

MUSIC PLUGGER: London loved this
little number last year.

[FIRST STAGEHAND *brings on a cloud,
and puts it in place.*]

FIRST STAGEHAND: Can't find the other
clouds, Mr Trafford.

TRAFFORD: [*over his shoulder*] Blown
away, have they?

FIRST STAGEHAND: Looks like it.

[*He exits.*]

TRAFFORD: [*shouting awkwardly over
his shoulder*] Did you try behind the
Cobb and Co. coach?

MUSIC PLUGGER: Perhaps I should come
back another time.

TRAFFORD: No, no, Miss Smallgood.
Play on. I'm giving you my divided
attention.

[SECOND STAGEHAND *brings on a
chair and places it beside the throne.*]

SEAMSTRESS: Arms higher, please, Your
Highness.

[*A* WORKER *wheels on a barrow full
of rubble.*]

TRAFFORD: What's this? I told you to
use the side door.

WORKER: We've boarded up the side
door, Guv.

TRAFFORD: You can't bring that across
here.

[*The* WORKER *backs off with difficulty. Enter* OLD ACTRESS, THIRD
ACTRESS *and* ROSIE. *They carry
costumes.*]

ROSIE: They're knocking down the ladies' dressing room.

THIRD ACTRESS: There's a big hole in the wall.

TRAFFORD: My apologies, ladies. The old girl is undergoing a little internal surgery.

OLD ACTRESS: Where do we dress, then?

TRAFFORD: There's a new fire exit going through.

ROSIE: We should have the men's dressing room.

THIRD ACTRESS: Or perhaps you'd like us to dress in the street!

[*The* MUSIC PLUGGER *stops playing.*]

MUSIC PLUGGER: I think I shall go on to Her Majesty's. I expect they'll be more interested.

[*She exits.*]

TRAFFORD: Thank you, indeed, Miss Smallgood. Your playing is sheer delight.

ROSIE: All right, George. Don't tell us. We have to dress here. Is that it?

TRAFFORD: My dear splendid ladies. Have no fear. I shall turn the other way.

[*The* ACTRESSES *and* ROSIE *grumble and begin dressing.* STAGEHANDS *struggle on with two more chairs and several clouds which they place in position.*]

SEAMSTRESS: [*standing up*] There we are.

TRAFFORD: 'Through tatter'd clothes small vices do appear. Robes and furr'd gowns hide all'. Unfortunately I can't wear it all the time.

[*He whips off the robe and hands it to the* SEAMSTRESS.]

Please make sure it's right for tonight.

[*The* SEAMSTRESS *exits. Enter a* WORKER *pushing the wheelbarrow, accompanied by a* CONTRACTOR. *The* WORKER *crosses the stage and exits while the* CONTRACTOR *engages* TRAFFORD.]

TRAFFORD: It can't go across here.

CONTRACTOR: Mr Trafford. Please be reasonable. There's no alternative.

TRAFFORD: The contract states you will not disrupt the business of the theatre.

CONTRACTOR: And so we won't. We simply have to clear away some of the rubble.

TRAFFORD: Not across the stage, you don't.

[TRAFFORD *and the* CONTRACTOR *confront each other.*]

CONTRACTOR: We could always down tools. But I seem to recall something about a city building inspector's deadline.

[STAGEHANDS *carrying an enormous model of a bi-plane step between them, forcing them to step back. Wires descend and the* STAGEHANDS *hang it up centre stage. Enter a* NEWSBOY.]

NEWSBOY: Fursflydoversiddy! Fousanbounbryze! [*To* TRAFFORD] Wonnabuyabaybaguv?

[TRAFFORD *buys a paper. The* WORKER *re-enters with an empty barrow. The* NEWSBOY *sells some more papers and exits.*]

TRAFFORD: All right, Byles. I don't care what you do. Knock the whole side wall out if you have to. But get that vehicle off.

[*Exit the* CONTRACTOR *and* WORKER *with the barrow. Enter* ESSON.]

ESSON: Excuse me. Louis Esson.

TRAFFORD: [*reading his paper*] Sorry.
Don't know him.

ESSON: No. I'm Louis Esson.

TRAFFORD: Ah.

ESSON: I sent you a play.

TRAFFORD: Not now, please.

[*Enter the* SEAMSTRESS *with*
TRAFFORD's *Master of Ceremonies
costume. She helps him dress.*]

ESSON: Did you read it?

TRAFFORD: Sorry. We're very busy.

ESSON: It was about Australian politics.

TRAFFORD: Aren't these braces crossed?

ESSON: Louis Esson. I'm a journalist
and poet.

TRAFFORD: Mr Esson. I have not read
your play. Nor do I recall receiving
it. See that pile there? Those are the
successful plays of last year from
London and New York. I've not read
them either. In fact, there are
thousands of plays in the world.
Yours is but one. I am sorry to say so,
but it's probably on the bottom of the
pile.

ESSON: Well, in that case, it won't be
hard to find. Perhaps you'll give it
back to me.

TRAFFORD: If I had the time to find it,
I'm sure I would return it with
pleasure.

ESSON: Don't bother yourself. I'll get it.

[ESSON *moves towards the pile.*]

TRAFFORD: [*blocking his way*] Why
don't you come back on Monday?

ESSON: You told me to come back
today.

TRAFFORD: Did I, really? Please come
on Monday, Mr Esson. I shall see
what I can do then.

[ESSON *exits.*]

TRAFFORD: [*mimicking*] 'It's about
Australian politics'. [*Exasperated*]
Who'd bother writing a play about
that?

[*There is a crescendo of sound. They
all listen. It defines itself as that of an
aeroplane motor. The sound rises and
thunders overhead. Everyone crouches
somewhat. The sound passes over.*]

EVERYONE: [*variously*] He's up! He's
made it! He's done it!

TRAFFORD: He *has* done it, by golly.
[*Putting his top hat on his head*]
Open up out front! We're in business.

[*Blackout.*]

SCENE THREE.

*The stage as before. Fanfare.
Triumphant march. Streamers and
confetti. A procession enters led by the*
ACCOMPANIST *with a bass drum. The*
MAYOR *and a* NEWSPAPER MAGNATE
follow behind. The AVIATOR *is escorted
by* ROSIE *dressed as 'Winged Victory';
the* OLD ACTRESS *dressed as 'Britannia'
and* THIRD ACTRESS *dressed as
'Australia' as well as* TRAFFORD, *a*
REPORTER *and a* PHOTOGRAPHER. *The*
MAYOR *and the* MAGNATE *take seats.
The* AVIATOR *is shown to the throne.
'Winged Victory', 'Britannia' and
'Australia' form a tableau around him.*
TRAFFORD *comes forward. He raises his
arms to stop the continuing barrage of
streamers and applause.*

TRAFFORD: Ladies and gentlemen.
Welcome to the celebrations. We're
here to congratulate the conqueror
. . . to crown the King of the Clouds.
But first—the Lord Mayor.

[*The* MAYOR *comes forward to
applause. He adjusts his glasses on his
nose. Being almost illiterate, he reads
his speech with difficulty.*]

MAYOR: Dear citizens. This is a historic

moment for our fair city. A man has flown like a pig . . . er, pigeon. We have looked up and — [*turning the page*] . . . a wonderful sight, dear citizens. Surely it is a miracle of modern times. The city salutes you, Mr De Vries. And we give to you the key to her heart.

[*Applause.* TRAFFORD *produces the key in a plush box which the* MAYOR *fumblingly presents to the* AVIATOR. *The* NEWSPAPER MAGNATE *steps forward. He holds up a small case which he opens to great applause. It is full of banknotes.*]

MAGNATE: My Lord Mayor. Ladies and gentlemen. Well—what can I say? He's done it, and he's done it in style. On behalf of the *Daily News* and the *Evening Standard* I'm specially pleased to give the prize to Mr De Vries. This thousand pound's been on offer to any in the world. But it's an Australian who defied Australian gravity to take the first powered flight over the buildings of the city.

[*Cheers.*]

I reckon we've seen written in the sky this afternoon a message for the future: we're a great new nation, and we're headed for higher things.

[*Applause. He snaps the case shut with a bang and hands it to the* AVIATOR.]

MAGNATE: Good on you, mate.

[*Applause. Fireworks explode from the model plane overhead. The* ACTRESSES *and* ROSIE *come forward. They are joined by a* PLAYER PILOT *who soars in. The* ACCOMPANIST *strikes up on the piano. The* PLAYER PILOT *holds a huge key which he uses as a joystick.* ROSIE *clings to his arm. They sing and dance as a chorus line to the tune of the 'Can Can'.*]

ACTRESSES: When he was just a little fella,
Jumping with an umbrella,
Down he flapped, the little chap,
He hit the deck, well what the heck?
ROSIE: A few years later undeterred
He fashioned wings—a pretty bird.
ACTRESSES: He tried the wind, he took a spin,
He tumbled like a hurdy-gurdy.
PLAYER PILOT: But today I got it right,
I soared aloft in fancy flight.
ALL: Above the crowds, among the clouds.
PLAYER PILOT: I vanished out of sight. [*Tacet.*]
ALL: [*key change*] And . . . he . . . is . . .
Up! He's up! He's in the air,
He's Adam in the atmosphere.
Unprecedented, he's ascended.
TRAFFORD: [*bass*] First into the firmament.
ALL: He's up! He's up! He's in the air,
He's done it with such dashing flare.
PLAYER PILOT: I tell no lies, I closed my eyes.
ALL: He landed over there. Hey!

[*The music speeds up. The* PLAYER PILOT, ACTRESSES, ROSIE *and* TRAFFORD *dance a vigorous can-can. Applause.*]

TRAFFORD: Thank you, ladies and gentlemen. I expect you're looking forward—as I am eagerly—to hearing Mr De Vries' own account of his momentous flight.

[*The* AVIATOR *is brought forward.*]

What is it like, sir, to soar there so high and free? Can you tell the man in the street what it's really like to fly?

[*As* TRAFFORD *speaks the*
PHOTOGRAPHER *moves his camera to
the front. He gets under the cloth
and holds up the pan. The* REPORTER
*moves forward, pen poised. Then all
stand in tableau waiting for the*
AVIATOR *to speak. The* AVIATOR
*opens his mouth. He tries for words,
shakes his head. He tries again.*]

AVIATOR: It was . . . indescribable.

[*There is a blinding white flash in the*
PHOTOGRAPHER'*s pan. Blackout.*]

SCENE FOUR

*Not long after the previous scene. The
stage is being cleared of the props. The
throne is to stay.* ROSIE *sits on the
throne taking off her shoes and
stockings. During this scene she and*
TRAFFORD *take off their costumes of the
previous scene and put on Shake-
spearean outfits. The* CARETAKER
WOMAN *sweeps up piles of confetti and
streamers.* STAGEHANDS *remove props.
Eventually a backcloth will descend
depicting the battle-field at Agincourt.
The model bi-plane is not removed
until the end of the scene.*

ROSIE: I don't see the point, George.

TRAFFORD: It's simpler. It's the best
solution.

ROSIE: This damned theatre. You live
and breathe it. It's unhealthy.

TRAFFORD: I have to keep an eye on
things.

[*He exits, then re-enters, pulling his
desk on stage. On it are papers and a
handset telephone.*]

ROSIE: Sleeping here. It's ridiculous.

TRAFFORD: There's so much to do.
Besides, I'm writing a new play.

ROSIE: My place would be quieter. For
writing.

TRAFFORD: I can't move in there. You'd
distract me. Look. I'm fine. I have a
bed . . . a stretcher. It gets private
enough here after midnight.

ROSIE: The bloody theatre.

TRAFFORD: Oh. Language, young
lady.

ROSIE: I'll say bloody if I want to.
It's modern for women.
[*Pause.*]

TRAFFORD: Say it again.

ROSIE: What?

TRAFFORD: Bloody.

ROSIE: [*puckering up, writhing
seductively and in a comic, deep,
sensual voice*] Bllloody.

TRAFFORD: [*flinging himself on top of
her on the throne*] What an
inspiration!

[*Enter the* NEWSPAPER MAGNATE
*puffing on a cigar and carrying a
bottle of champagne. He looks away,
embarrassed. He works at the cork of
the bottle.*]

MAGNATE: Congratulations, Trafford.
I reckon we deserve a party, don't
you?

[TRAFFORD *struggles from* ROSIE *and
goes for glasses from the drawer of
the desk.*]

You were a delight, my dear.

[ROSIE *crosses her legs. The* MAGNATE
splutters on his cigar.]

A veritable delight. By gum.

ROSIE: Thank you, Mr Townsend. You
weren't bad yourself.

[*The* MAGNATE *glows. He can't keep
his eyes off her.*]

MAGNATE: Sydney's jumping, George.
They're dancing all down Pitt Street.
And that aviator. What a bloke! The
women are tearing his clothes off.

[*He pops the champagne cork.* ROSIE
re-crosses her legs.]
Ha, ha. Half his luck.

ROSIE: I thought he was a dope.

MAGNATE: Ah. Come on.

[*The* MAGNATE *begins pouring the
drinks.*]

TRAFFORD: He's a hero.

MAGNATE: The strong, silent type. An
Australian hero.

TRAFFORD: Though I do wish he'd said
more. People want to know what it's
like up there, don't they?

MAGNATE: He was perfect. Didn't make
a fool of himself by prattling on.

ROSIE: He was scared.

TRAFFORD: [*raising his glass, with an
eye on the bi-plane overhead*] To the
aviator!

MAGNATE: [*raising his glass*] Adam in
the atmosphere!

ROSIE: [*as the men clink their glasses
and drink*] He was still shaking.
[*Pause.*]
He was tumescent.

TRAFFORD: Eh?

MAGNATE: [*spluttering*] Steady on.

ROSIE: It was fear.

MAGNATE: You actresses.

ROSIE: Didn't you see it?

TRAFFORD: I wasn't looking.

ROSIE: It was his fear rising.

MAGNATE: No doubt about the world of
the theatre. No inhibitions. Say it like
you see it.

ROSIE: I can't help it if I noticed.

TRAFFORD: It's not what we expect from
heroes, is it!
[*The* MAGNATE *drains his glass.*]

MAGNATE: He's already in history. He's
a hero no matter what happens in his
pants. I reckon there must be ten
thousand celebrating him out there.
Probably twenty thousand. It's been a
wonderful day.
[*He takes a big cheque book from his
pocket and starts writing.*]
And you've done a splendid job,
George. A perfect reception.

TRAFFORD: Glad to be of help, Frank.

MAGNATE: [*writing*] By the way, I don't
suppose you've thought about
diversifying a little, have you? This
place would make a fine moving
picture palace.

TRAFFORD: Not the old Empire. Live
theatre's our business here.

MAGNATE: Shakespeare and bushrangers? Pah! Melodrama's dead. It's
just not buried yet.
[MOLLY *enters behind.*]

TRAFFORD: I have a vision for the
theatre, Frank—

MAGNATE: Oh, well. They do call you
the King of Melodrama, don't they?
[*Handing over the cheque*] There you
are, my friend.
[*They shake hands.*]

MOLLY: What's this about visions,
George? You still having them?

MAGNATE: Ah! Mrs Trafford! The city's
leading lady! It's so good to see you
again.

MOLLY: Hello, Frank. It's nice to know
my work still has one admirer.

MAGNATE: How could I ever forget?

MOLLY: Hello, Rosie.

TRAFFORD: Get out. You're trespassing.

MOLLY: Don't be boring, George.

MAGNATE: Your performance in that
Swede's play . . . you know—*The
Dolly House*. Superb.

ROSIE: Norwegian. Ibsen was a
Norwegian.

MAGNATE: That Nora. You had her down to a T.

MOLLY: I worked hard on her.

TRAFFORD: I wish you wouldn't come round here bothering us, Molly. It's embarrassing having to throw you out the back door.

MAGNATE: Surely you don't do that!

MOLLY: He gets the stagehands to do it. He wouldn't touch me himself.

TRAFFORD: You no longer have a place here.

MOLLY: So you say. But where would you be without me, I wonder? Who established this company's reputation? Who set this theatre alight with applause and curtain calls?

TRAFFORD: We were a team, remember?

MOLLY: They poured champagne over me. They mobbed me at the stage door.

TRAFFORD: I wrote your best parts.

MOLLY: And I rewrote them so they made sense.

MAGNATE: [mediating] Yes. Vitality was what you two had. Energy. Electricity. What a pair you were!

TRAFFORD: Good acting, it was.

MOLLY: Oh, deny it as much as you like. Your plays were indulgent nonsense. Melodramatic clap-trap. The full houses were there for me.

TRAFFORD: For my writing. My ideas.

MOLLY: [scathingly] Your ideas about what?

TRAFFORD: Well, about . . .

MOLLY: Lost for words?

MAGNATE: Your plays had great popular appeal, George. They made money.

MOLLY: We sucked it out of them. They loved it. They loved me.

TRAFFORD: [to MOLLY] God, you're an ugly woman.

MOLLY: Because I tell the truth? You find the truth ugly, don't you.

MAGNATE: Ahem. I was just leaving. [Taking MOLLY by the arm] You don't mind if I escort your wife away for a little drink, do you?

TRAFFORD: Do what you like with her.

[The MAGNATE and MOLLY head off.]

MOLLY: [to TRAFFORD] Don't think you'll ever get rid of me. I may be separated from you; but I'm married to this theatre.

MAGNATE: [to MOLLY as they leave] Let me tell you about the film industry, Mrs Trafford. Plenty of opportunity there.

[The MAGNATE and MOLLY exit.]

ROSIE: She was upset.

TRAFFORD: She's living in the past. She won't accept the world is changing.

ROSIE: And you do?

TRAFFORD: I'm helping it to change.

ROSIE: You baulked at Frank's talk of moving pictures—of turning this place into a cinematographe.

TRAFFORD: Well, of course, I did. My vision is for live theatre. I want live theatre to move with the times. I want to capture the romance of the new century here on the stage. There's a new man emerging: twentieth-century man. He's coming from within. He's a god, you understand. He moves at the speed of sound. He communicates by invisible wires. He puts a girdle round the earth in forty minutes—literally. He's there inside us, preparing to break free. I see him dressed in flying suit, cap and goggles, waiting for his flight. That's why the aviator was such a let down this afternoon. He didn't say a thing. He *is* the new century's man. He's *been* up there. But he didn't tell anybody what it's like. He didn't *free* the man in anyone else. I'm going to write a play that does just that. I'll set the new man free in everybody.

ROSIE: The cinematographe might do it better.

TRAFFORD: Poh. I thought you shared my faith in theatre.

ROSIE: I acknowledge its limitations.

TRAFFORD: I don't acknowledge any limitations.

ROSIE: Perhaps you should.

TRAFFORD: Nobody gets anywhere acknowledging limitations.

ROSIE: [*smiling and shaking her head*] You're crazy. No wonder I love you. But do you realise you've robbed the world of one of its great celebrities?

TRAFFORD: Who's that?

ROSIE: Me! If I hadn't fallen in love with you, I would have been a great expeditionary: a lone woman adventurer. I would have travelled unescorted to New Guinea, Africa, South America. First white woman into the interior! Intrepid female among the cannibals! If you hadn't waylaid me I'd be famous by now.

TRAFFORD: Are you sorry?

ROSIE: Not at all. I find exploring the dark corners of you sufficiently dangerous.

TRAFFORD: You flatter me. My exciting dark corners!

ROSIE: They don't in themselves excite.

TRAFFORD: Oh.

ROSIE: But the chance of discovering El Dorado there does.

TRAFFORD: El Dorado?

ROSIE: The golden man.

TRAFFORD: I thought El Dorado was a place.

ROSIE: You should read more. El Dorado was a man. He wore only gold. He had to hide from the Conquistadors. Men still go out looking for him. Or at least for the gold he wore. See here.

[*She takes up a newspaper and reads.*]

'An expedition, led by the celebrated British engineer W. Cooper, set off for the Peruvian interior last week. Mr Cooper plans to drain Lake Guatavita using a patented steam pump. In the mud of the lake's bottom, it is believed, lies the fabulous El Dorado treasure.'

[*She throws aside the newspaper.*]

Beautiful, isn't it? A golden man undressing and throwing the gold away. Every year. And every year re-clothed in new gold.

TRAFFORD: [*laughing*] I'm not likely to be divesting myself of any gold, I'm afraid.

ROSIE: In your case I'm speaking metaphorically.

TRAFFORD: I've been exploring my interior for years. There are still great blanks on the map. Perhaps the play I'm about to write will discover something. An inland sea, maybe.

ROSIE: Your play about flying?

TRAFFORD: Yes. Exploration from the air it will be. From up there you can see all the way to the horizons.

ROSIE: Clouds and thin air.

TRAFFORD: You see the total geography.

ROSIE: But none of its details.

TRAFFORD: To know yourself you have to be liberated from yourself.

ROSIE: But not leave yourself behind.

[*Pause.* TRAFFORD *shrugs, then puts his head in his hands.*]

Besides, when have you ever flown?

TRAFFORD: [*vehemently*] I will. Don't you worry.

[*The phone rings.* TRAFFORD *grabs it angrily.* ROSIE *continues to undress.*]

Trafford here . . . Walter! Where are you?

ROSIE: You should get that aviator to take you up.

TRAFFORD: [*into the phone*] Adrian? Well, get him out of there . . . Just bring him up here, Walter. We'll see if we can dry him out . . .

ROSIE: Actually, there's another legend that suits you better, George.

TRAFFORD: [*looking at his watch*] It's past the half hour call . . .

ROSIE: A more modern one. The story of Pinocchio.

TRAFFORD: Just hurry, will you! [*Putting the phone down, annoyed*] Why do they always build a pub next door to a theatre?

[*He continues to dress hurriedly.*]

ROSIE: Did you ever hear the story of Pinocchio?

TRAFFORD: The puppet boy?

ROSIE: Pulled by many strings he was. Remained wooden until he learned to be unselfish. And to love.

TRAFFORD: His nose kept growing long, didn't it?

ROSIE: Whenever he avoided the truth. Tumescence of the nasal organ.

[*Pause.* TRAFFORD *buckles on a sword.*]

TRAFFORD: What did you have to say that for?

ROSIE: What?

TRAFFORD: About the aviator. Frank's a little sensitive in those areas.

ROSIE: Oh. He's a hypocrite.

TRAFFORD: He's a rich hypocrite. He's our major backer. And he has been known to ensure we didn't get bad reviews.

ROSIE: When we deserved them?

[*The* OLD *and* YOUNG ACTORS *enter. The* YOUNG ACTOR *is drunk.*]

OLD ACTOR: Enter the Prologue.

TRAFFORD: [*sarcastically*] Wonderful. The true spirit of Shakespeare.

YOUNG ACTOR: 'O for a muse of . . . muse of fire . . .'

TRAFFORD: [*shouting over him*] Adrian! What's the big idea?

YOUNG ACTOR: That would ashcend the—

[*He burps.*]

TRAFFORD: [*shouting over him*] It's not just me you're letting down.

YOUNG ACTOR: . . . ashcend the—

[*He burps and vomits, narrowly missing* TRAFFORD.]

TRAFFORD: Ahhh. Get him out of here.

OLD ACTOR: What'll I do with him?

TRAFFORD: Throw him in the toilet.

OLD ACTOR: I found him in the toilet.

TRAFFORD: Well, throw him back.

[*The* ACTORS *exit.* TRAFFORD *looks at his watch, then at the pool of vomit. He is beginning to panic.*]

Dear God.

[*The* SEAMSTRESS *enters with the robe. She helps* TRAFFORD *into it.*]

ROSIE: I could do the Prologue.

TRAFFORD: You couldn't, could you? And the Chorus? You'll be doing some quick changes.

ROSIE: I'm used to that.

TRAFFORD: You're a doll.

[*The* SEAMSTRESS *exits.* TRAFFORD *kisses* ROSIE *hurriedly. He looks down*

to see he is standing in the pool of vomit. Shouting as he moves to off]
Someone come and clean this mess up! Quickly!
[*The* CARETAKER WOMAN *enters with bucket and mop.*]
[*Blackout.*]

SCENE FIVE

The wings left during a performance off right. The play is Henry V.
Two STAGEHANDS *stand by with props.*
FIRST STAGEHAND *smokes a cigar ostentatiously.*

FIRST STAGEHAND: It doesn't matter.

SECOND STAGEHAND: I reckon you ought to.

FIRST STAGEHAND: Get off. [*Peering off right*] What are they up to? It's a battle scene. See?

SECOND STAGEHAND: I reckon you'll cop it.

FIRST STAGEHAND: Smoke. See? It adds to the effect.

SECOND STAGEHAND: They've got plenty of smoke from that brazier sorter thing.

FIRST STAGEHAND: Bit more won't hurt.

SECOND STAGEHAND: It's unsafe.

FIRST STAGEHAND: That's what I reckon.

SECOND STAGEHAND: And you're still doing it!

FIRST STAGEHAND: The brazier, mug. It's unsafe.

SECOND STAGEHAND: These canvases burn like—

FIRST STAGEHAND: I'm not going to toss the butt down into them.

SECOND STAGEHAND: They do. Like bloody billy-o.

FIRST STAGEHAND: I'm being careful, aren't I?

SECOND STAGEHAND: Like blazes.

FIRST STAGEHAND: Gawd struth.
[*He tosses the cigar down.*]

SECOND STAGEHAND: [*jumping*] Watch it.
[*He stamps on the butt.*]

FIRST STAGEHAND: Couldn't have a quiet smoke round here if you tried. [*He sulks.*]

SECOND STAGEHAND: I never knew you smoked.

FIRST STAGEHAND: I don't. Can't afford it.

SECOND STAGEHAND: Didn't think so. [*Pause.*]

FIRST STAGEHAND: Bloke was giving them away.

SECOND STAGEHAND: What bloke?

FIRST STAGEHAND: Down the Quay. Aviator's mate.

SECOND STAGEHAND: You down the Quay?

FIRST STAGEHAND: Helped pitch him in, I did.

SECOND STAGEHAND: The bloke?

FIRST STAGEHAND: The aviator.

SECOND STAGEHAND: In the harbour, sorter thing?

FIRST STAGEHAND: End of the Manly ferry wharf.

SECOND STAGEHAND: What did you pitch him in for?

FIRST STAGEHAND: *I* didn't pitch him in. There was hundreds of us.

SECOND STAGEHAND: The aviator?

FIRST STAGEHAND: Traditional, ain't it?

SECOND STAGEHAND: Not traditional.

FIRST STAGEHAND: Too right, it is.

SECOND STAGEHAND: How can it be?

FIRST STAGEHAND: Always do it.

SECOND STAGEHAND: He's the first.

FIRST STAGEHAND: It's traditional to pitch the captain into the harbour.

SECOND STAGEHAND: Not a captain.

FIRST STAGEHAND: 'Course he is.

SECOND STAGEHAND: Wasn't a boat race.

FIRST STAGEHAND: Good as.

[Pause.]

SECOND STAGEHAND: How many cigars this bloke give away?

FIRST STAGEHAND: Dozens.

SECOND STAGEHAND: Blimey.

FIRST STAGEHAND: And they had to fish him out in the end.

SECOND STAGEHAND: The bloke?

FIRST STAGEHAND: The aviator. Couldn't swim.

SECOND STAGEHAND: Could fly but he couldn't swim?

FIRST STAGEHAND: Reckon.

SECOND STAGEHAND: Had them big flying boots on.

FIRST STAGEHAND: Nah. Couldn't swim.

SECOND STAGEHAND: Not even dog-paddle?

FIRST STAGEHAND: Sank a few times.

SECOND STAGEHAND: Get away.

FIRST STAGEHAND: Everyone was laughing.

SECOND STAGEHAND: Poor bugger.

FIRST STAGEHAND: Bobbed under a few times. Put the old hand up in the air.

SECOND STAGEHAND: Must of been drowning.

FIRST STAGEHAND: 'Woo woo', he was going.

SECOND STAGEHAND: Must of been drowning.

FIRST STAGEHAND: [peering off right] 'Struth. Scene change.

[He exits. The OLD and the YOUNG ACTRESS enter in Elizabethan costume and cross.]

OLD ACTRESS: I hate the theatre.

YOUNG ACTRESS: Did you see what he was doing to me, Alice?

OLD ACTRESS: I hate acting as much as I hate old actors.

YOUNG ACTRESS: He had his sword poking between my legs.

OLD ACTRESS: We'll get him back in the fifth act.

[They exit. FIRST STAGEHAND returns, pushing the throne.]

FIRST STAGEHAND: So. Where was I?

SECOND STAGEHAND: The aviator. In the drink. Drowning, sorter thing.

FIRST STAGEHAND: [aggressively] Well, I wasn't going in after him.

SECOND STAGEHAND: Why not?

FIRST STAGEHAND: And get me cigar wet? Worth threepence, that cigar.

SECOND STAGEHAND: I reckon.

FIRST STAGEHAND: Besides. Had to fight for it. Thousands of blokes there. Cost me a couple of pretty hefty blows to the side of the head.

SECOND STAGEHAND: Hurt you?

FIRST STAGEHAND: Nah. Other bloke's head. I knocked it out of his mouth.

[Pause.]

SECOND STAGEHAND: Reckon it was imported?

FIRST STAGEHAND: Might of been.

SECOND STAGEHAND: Worth sixpence, the overseas job.

FIRST STAGEHAND: Well. It was a good 'un, all right.

[Pause.]

SECOND STAGEHAND: [bending down] Where'd it go?

FIRST STAGEHAND: No good now.

SECOND STAGEHAND: Might be OK, sorter thing.

FIRST STAGEHAND: Nah. It's buggered.

SECOND STAGEHAND: Here it is.

FIRST STAGEHAND: Looks pretty buggered.

SECOND STAGEHAND: Got a match?

FIRST STAGEHAND: You're an optimist.

SECOND STAGEHAND: Come on.

[*He lights it.*]

FIRST STAGEHAND: There you go.

SECOND STAGEHAND: Not bad.

[*He coughs.*]

Imported.

FIRST STAGEHAND: How would you know?

[HIGGS *has entered. He snatches the cigar from* SECOND STAGEHAND's *mouth and tosses it down, stepping on it.*]

HIGGS: You'll cop it.

SECOND STAGEHAND: I was being careful.

HIGGS: Those canvases burn like billy-o.

FIRST STAGEHAND: He wasn't going to toss the butt down into them.

HIGGS: It's against the regulations.

SECOND STAGEHAND: Just having a quiet smoke.

HIGGS: Why do you think they're putting in new fire exits, eh?

FIRST STAGEHAND: Was a celebration.

HIGGS: It's a bloody death trap, this place.

SECOND STAGEHAND: It was only a little celebration, sorter thing.

HIGGS: I'd hate to be in it if it went up.

SECOND STAGEHAND: The aviator. First flight, it was.

HIGGS: You blokes ought to know better. Should report you.

FIRST STAGEHAND: Come on, Higgsy. Give us a break.

HIGGS: All right. Anyway . . . [*grinning*] . . . just put one out meself.

FIRST STAGEHAND: You get one too?

HIGGS: I got five.

SECOND STAGEHAND: Blimey.

FIRST STAGEHAND: How'd you get five?

HIGGS: Didn't knock over any old fellas.

FIRST STAGEHAND: I bet.

[*Pause.*]

HIGGS: Listen. Are you blokes ready for tonight?

FIRST STAGEHAND: I reckon.

SECOND STAGEHAND: What do we have to do?

HIGGS: Stick around after the curtain.

FIRST STAGEHAND: The big showdown, eh? Ambush Trafford.

SECOND STAGEHAND: Bail 'im up, sorter thing.

HIGGS: We're only after what's rightly owed us.

FIRST STAGEHAND: There'll be a blue, betcha.

HIGGS: It's justice we're after. Not a fight.

FIRST STAGEHAND: He's a sly bastard.

SECOND STAGEHAND: He can play-act his way round you.

FIRST STAGEHAND: He can be looking you in the eye, but you know he's sidling round behind you at the same time.

HIGGS: We can handle him. He's all bluff. The facts are there for all to see in our pay packets.

FIRST STAGEHAND: He's a tight bastard, all right.

SECOND STAGEHAND: He's starving us.

HIGGS: He's conveniently forgotten there's such a thing as a basic wage now. We'll just have to remind him.

SECOND STAGEHAND: Are we getting it—the basic wage, sorter thing?

FIRST STAGEHAND: You must be joking.

HIGGS: We will be getting it. Now, this action tonight, if it fails, we go further. Who says the golden age of unionism's a thing of the past, eh?

FIRST STAGEHAND: Good on you, Higgsy. Go for broke.

HIGGS: Just make sure you're there to back me up.

FIRST STAGEHAND: We're behind you, mate.

SECOND STAGEHAND: Yeah, mate.

[HIGGS *begins to exit.*]

Hey, Higgsy. How many of them cigars you got left?

[HIGGS *shows four from his pocket.*]

HIGGS: You'll be smoking them with me tonight, right? Just back me up.

[*Blackout.*]

SCENE SIX

The wings right. MOLLY *enters alone. Henry V has just concluded off left. Applause is heard.* MOLLY *peers off left. She is visibly annoyed. From the shouts and applause it is clear the performance went reasonably well.* MOLLY *turns to a board of electrical meters behind her. She pulls down the handle of a large switch. Sparks fly. Shouts from left: 'Hey!' 'Lights', 'A blackout', etc.* MOLLY *retires into the darkness.* FIRST STAGEHAND *rushes on, fumbles at the board, then in a shower of sparks turns the lights back on. Fresh, louder applause from off left.*

The puzzled STAGEHAND *looks at the board for a moment, then exits right.* MOLLY *re-emerges, pleased with herself. A* SOLICITOR *enters behind her in the dim light.*

SOLICITOR: Mrs Trafford? John Hope.

MOLLY: [*startled*] Oh. John.

SOLICITOR: They said I'd find you here.

MOLLY: Yes. Old habits die hard. Some mornings I wake up in a panic thinking I have to get here for a matinée. Several times I've come all the way to the stage door—in a kind of trance, I suppose—expecting my dressing-room to be cleaned, my costume waiting, my role ready to be played. There used to be fresh flowers by my mirror every day. Red flowers. Only ever red . . .

SOLICITOR: I think I understand.

MOLLY: I'm told the old times are over. I don't accept that. The past is never dead, is it?

SOLICITOR: Well, as your family solicitor I suggest you take with you as much of that past as you can.

MOLLY: 'Take with me'?

SOLICITOR: Your husband wants to divorce you, doesn't he?

MOLLY: Yes. I have no objection to a fair settlement.

SOLICITOR: *Matrimonial Causes Act, 1899.* As your solicitor I suggest you don't stick around.

MOLLY: What?

SOLICITOR: It's a man's world, the world of the law. If your husband doesn't want you he can dispose of you like any other property.

MOLLY: I'd like to see him try.

SOLICITOR: He can trump up a charge of adultery against you. I know of several professional co-respondents

who hire themselves out as witnesses.
They can produce the most lurid
details in the box.

MOLLY: Professional perjury?

SOLICITOR: And you're at a further
disadvantage being an actress. You
are a woman with your own career.
The court won't look favourably upon
that. The statistics show that actresses
are the group of women with the
highest rate of divorce. Because they
are independent of their husbands in
the area of income, the court has no
pity on them.

MOLLY: But I own this theatre. Half
of it's mine. I built up its reputation.
I paid off its debts.

SOLICITOR: You and Mr Trafford did.

MOLLY: Yes.

SOLICITOR: *Ergo:* it's all his.

MOLLY: It is not.

SOLICITOR: *Matrimonial Causes Act,
1899.*

MOLLY: What about my house?

SOLICITOR: His house.

MOLLY: What about my child?

SOLICITOR: His child.

MOLLY: It can't be!

SOLICITOR: *Matrimonial Causes . . .*

MOLLY: Blast that! I'll not give up my
son! I'll not give up anything!

SOLICITOR: You'll have to.

MOLLY: I'll not give up the past.
George, yes, of course. But not what's
mine.

SOLICITOR: I'm sorry. As your family
solicitor, I can only advise the
following. One. You must hide the
child, stick him in a box or cupboard
somewhere, do anything you like but
don't let your husband know where
he is. Two. Change the locks on the
house. It helps in preventing your
private life becoming known to your
husband. Three. You must burn this
theatre down—

MOLLY: What?

SOLICITOR: It's the only way round
Matrimonial Causes Act, 1899. If the
theatre is in both your names you are
entitled to insurance monies after
divorce even though not to the
property itself. It's a fine point of law
. . . but I guarantee its success . . .

MOLLY: I can't do that. The Empire?
It's like home to me.

SOLICITOR: Four. Disappear. Smuggle
the child out and go. To some other
city. Take a new name. Start a new
life. It's the best advice I can offer.
Otherwise you lose everything.

[*Blackout.*]

SCENE SEVEN

*The stage after the performance.
Backcloth: the battle-field at Agincourt.
The throne sits empty at one side.*
HIGGS *stands on a large wooden crate
surrounded by the* ACTING TROUPE. *The*
YOUNG ACTOR *sits, head in hands.*
ROSIE *sits at the back. The* CARETAKER
WOMAN *scrubs floor.*

HIGGS: You've got to support us. If it
gets rough, you've got to come out
with us.

OLD ACTRESS: What do you mean 'come
out with you'?

OLD ACTOR: Not to the pub, love.

OLD ACTRESS: That's what going on
strike usually means.

HIGGS: There's a boom in entertainment. There are twenty-nine theatres
in this city—

OLD ACTOR: Isn't that the problem?

HIGGS: You've got to stake your claims.

OLD ACTRESS: Politics'll be the death of the theatre.

HIGGS: Oh? Starvation's essential for artistic integrity, is it?

OLD ACTRESS: My husband—God rest his skinny soul—once played Ned Kelly at the Garrick. One night when he fell down in a dead faint of hunger during the siege scene he received a standing ovation. One is not normally so lucky. It's the major qualification for an actor on the Australian stage: being able to survive for long periods with no food.

HIGGS: I see no virtue in that. You're all just workers like us stagehands.

OLD ACTOR: It's only other theatres will benefit if we disrupt performances here.

HIGGS: Don't you fellas have any principles? Or opinions?

OLD ACTOR: We have our standards.

HIGGS: And you're willing to trade them for poverty! If you go on working for peanuts you're prostituting yourselves and your standards. Political inactivity is a spreading disease. It rots the moral fabric; it eats away at principles. It's as bad as syphilis and alcoholism.

YOUNG ACTOR: You're a wowser, Higgs.

OLD ACTRESS: You'd have the theatre die of boredom.

OLD ACTOR: Your father was a Methodist, wasn't he? I knew him. I'm surprised you exist at all.

HIGGS: The trouble with you actors is . . . everything's just a play, isn't it? The true heroes of this country—God rest their skinny souls too—were shot by troopers' bullets in the shearers' strikes. They didn't get up to play the next night's performance!

OLD ACTOR: Is that the attraction of going on strike: martyrdom?

HIGGS: OK. Stay crawling in the slime. Don't let me be responsible for raising you out of it!

[HIGGS *exits.* STAGEHANDS *enter with a trolley.*]

SECOND STAGEHAND: Stand back, please.

[STAGEHANDS *lift onto the trolley the wooden crate* HIGGS *stood on.* 'INFLAMMABLE GOODS' *is stencilled on the crate in big letters and* 'EMPIRE TH. PITT' *is printed by hand in chalk.*]

YOUNG ACTRESS: What's in the box?

FIRST STAGEHAND: Coloured fire. Chemicals.

SECOND STAGEHAND: For the battle scenes.

YOUNG ACTOR: The stuff Australians come to the theatre to see. Explosions. Fireworks.

OLD ACTRESS: They certainly don't come to see acting.

YOUNG ACTRESS: They come for the blood.

[*The* STAGEHANDS *lean against the crate, waylaid by the talk.*]

OLD ACTRESS: Oh yes. The Australian imagination is wonderfully Gothic. It loves guts. Squash anything, give it a real beating, make it ooze, they applaud like mad. Especially if it's a person being squashed.

YOUNG ACTOR: Mm. I don't know. Furry animals go down well. Squish a wombat, or a wallaby. That gets them excited. Beat a koala to a pulp. Best of all, mash a mother kangaroo so the joey comes squelching out of the pocket . . . *plurrp!*

[*The* STAGEHANDS *laugh.*]

YOUNG ACTRESS: [*holding her stomach*] Do you mind!

YOUNG ACTOR: [*embracing her*]
Sorry, love.

OLD ACTRESS: How's it going?

YOUNG ACTRESS: [*feeling her stomach*]
Dreadful.

OLD ACTRESS: You'll be right. The first
is the worst.

YOUNG ACTRESS: But what'll happen
when I'm out here? We can't afford
for me to stop working.

OLD ACTRESS: Young Adrian'll have to
pull his socks up, won't he?
[*Chucking him under the chin*] Work
harder!

YOUNG ACTOR: Cut it out, Alice.

YOUNG ACTRESS: Him, pull his socks
up? He's always too busy pulling my
pants down.

YOUNG ACTOR: Hey, wait a minute—

OLD ACTRESS: Marriage isn't all beer
and skittles, my boy.

YOUNG ACTRESS: I'm the skittle!

YOUNG ACTOR: [*protesting*] We were
following the pamphlets from the
Neo-Malthusian society.

YOUNG ACTRESS: They didn't work.

OLD ACTRESS: The only way they work
is to hold them between your knees.

FIRST STAGEHAND: Ah, what are you
talking about! Everybody wants kids.

YOUNG ACTRESS: You'd be surprised.

FIRST STAGEHAND: It's a sin not to want
kids. Look at Queen Victoria, God
rest her teeming loins. She set an
example.

OLD ACTRESS: She set a blistering pace.

FIRST STAGEHAND: Nine kids in all. And
she was only four foot eleven.

OLD ACTOR: She had a plaster cast
made of Prince Albert's hand so she
could take it to bed with her after he
died.

YOUNG ACTRESS: Perhaps we could get a
plaster cast made of you. It'd be
safer.

YOUNG ACTOR: Of my hand?
[*Enter* TRAFFORD *dressed as Henry V.
He sees the crate.*]

TRAFFORD: What's this? Put it
somewhere safe.

[STAGEHANDS *wheel the crate off.*]

FIRST STAGEHAND: Yes, sir!

OLD ACTRESS: We were just leaving.

TRAFFORD: Goodnight, all.

[*The* TROUPE *exits.* ROSIE *remains.*]

ROSIE: [*quietly*] What are you doing
tonight?

TRAFFORD: [*biting his lip*] I can't.
Business.

ROSIE: Goodnight, then.

[ROSIE *exits.* TRAFFORD *throws himself
onto the throne. He looks exhausted.*
HIGGS *and the* STAGEHANDS *enter.*
TRAFFORD *changes his pose.*]

TRAFFORD: [*menacingly*] Goodnight,
gentlemen.

HIGGS: Ahem. Sir, it has come to the
attention of my fellow workers and
myself that the rates of pay in this
establishment are not consistent with
the requirements of the new
Commonwealth legislation relating to
a minimum wage for male employees
in industries comparable to this one
as supported by recent decisions of
the Arbitration Court presided over
by Justice Henry Bourne Higgins.

TRAFFORD: I don't pay you enough.
Is that it?

HIGGS: Please let me finish, sir. Ahem.
In the sausage skin industry the
minimum weekly award has been set
down at two pounds one and
tenpence for the family man working
the normal six day week. In the

artificial flower industry it is one pound eighteen shillings. We consider the value of our work to lie in the region of these industry figures seeing as how there's both labouring and creative components in the job we do. His Honour Mr Higgins has concluded that the newly referred to 'basic wage' be set at two pounds two shillings.

TRAFFORD: So? What are you after?

HIGGS: Ahem. Two pounds, sir.

TRAFFORD: Two pounds?

SECOND STAGEHAND: It's not even a basic wage.

TRAFFORD: There's no such thing as a basic wage. Who is this Justice Higgins? Some socialist hiding under a wig plucking figures from the air. It's easy for him to say this or that a week.

HIGGS: So what are you offering, sir?

TRAFFORD: Offering? If I have to increase your pay at all, it will be to . . . one pound ten.

HIGGS: An extra one and ninepence?

TRAFFORD: I can hardly afford that.

HIGGS: It's not what you can afford, sir. It's what a man's worth in the world. And what it costs to keep a wife and family. That's the idea of a basic wage.

TRAFFORD: It doesn't work as an argument, Higgs.

HIGGS: They get one pound fifteen in the ice cream industry! [*Disgusted*] A *woman* gets one pound three and fourpence making corsets!

TRAFFORD: Go and make corsets, then.

FIRST STAGEHAND: [*threateningly*] Do you know how much a loaf of bread costs, Mr Trafford? Well, do you?

SECOND STAGEHAND: [*equally threateningly*] Fivepence ha'penny. [*They fire off the facts like gunshots.*]

FIRST STAGEHAND: Or a pound of tea?

SECOND STAGEHAND: One and a penny ha'penny!

FIRST STAGEHAND: Sugar?

SECOND STAGEHAND: Tuppence ha'penny a pound!

FIRST STAGEHAND: Butter?

SECOND STAGEHAND: One and a penny ha'penny!

FIRST STAGEHAND: Pork?

SECOND STAGEHAND: Sevenpence three farthings!

FIRST STAGEHAND: [*bludgeoning*] Australian ale, threepence a pint!

SECOND STAGEHAND: [*stridently*] Tobacco, six and six a pound! [TRAFFORD *stands up on the throne, retreating from the attack.*]

FIRST STAGEHAND: Steak, eightpence three farthings!

SECOND STAGEHAND: Honey, fivepence a pound!

FIRST STAGEHAND: Eggs, one and fourpence ha'penny a dozen! [TRAFFORD *spreads his arms so that in his robe he looks like a great bird of prey.*]

SECOND STAGEHAND: Milk, fourpence three farthings!

FIRST STAGEHAND: Mutton, fourpence ha'penny!

SECOND STAGEHAND: Soap, threepence— [TRAFFORD *draws his property rapier and leaps from the throne directly onto the group of* STAGEHANDS.]

TRAFFORD: Aaaaarrrgh!

[*The* STAGEHANDS *scatter.* TRAFFORD *chases them until they have exited.*

HIGGS *remains motionless.* TRAFFORD
returns and slumps on the throne.
Pause. HIGGS *continues motionless,*
staring ahead.]
  Well?
HIGGS: Two pounds.
TRAFFORD: I can't afford it.
HIGGS: Have a heart, sir.
TRAFFORD: That I do have.
HIGGS: Does it beat, sir?
TRAFFORD: More than you could ever
  know, Higgs.
HIGGS: Two pounds is fair and just.
  [*Pause.*]
TRAFFORD: Let me tell you a story.
HIGGS: [*shaking his head*] Two pounds,
  sir.
TRAFFORD: [*a clever act*] Once upon a
  time — thirty years ago it was — there
  was a little bloke in a circus family.
  He used to . . . shovel up the
  elephant shit, wash out the wombat's
  waggon, give the monkey its milk,
  clean the clown's shoes, paint the
  ponies, brush the baboon. It was . . .
  a job. But times weren't good. The
  banks were heading for one of their
  crashes. The crowds were getting
  fewer. It wasn't expensive entertainment. It was ha'pennies and three-
  pences at the door. We went longer
  and longer distances to more and
  more isolated towns. Eventually the
  audiences were let in free of charge.
  We'd have had none otherwise. And
  meantime the troupe dwindled from
  a dozen to six to two. My father and
  his mate were the ones left. My father
  was a short chap; the other bloke was
  tall. Six foot six. Together they
  played a full programme. The posters
  showed a whole variety: Apollo and
  Mercury — equestrians; David and
  Goliath — gymnasts; Atlas and

Sisyphus — jugglers; Aboo and the
Maharajah — clown act with elephant.
They played nights and matinées.
They never skipped a routine. They
never short-shirted the programme no
matter how small the crowd. And you
know what those crowds did? Those
crowds that had been let in free?
They'd pay on the way out. Never
anyone collecting, mind you. They'd
just throw down their money at the
tent flap and go. They were generous
because the entertainment they'd
been given was generous. Entertainment is a generous industry, Higgs.
Its always has been. And it's brought
out generosity in those it has
influenced and supported.
[*Pause.*]
If I could pay you more I would.
[*Pause.*]
HIGGS: [*looking unflinchingly ahead*]
Two pounds, sir. It's not unjust.
[TRAFFORD *stands. He faces* HIGGS,
*sharply lifts the sword and holds its
point at* HIGGS' *throat.*]
TRAFFORD: One pound ten. It's what I
can afford.
[*Pause. Slowly* HIGGS *pushes the
sword point aside with a forefinger,
then gives it a disdainful flick down.*]
HIGGS: [*threateningly*] You'll hear
further from us, Mr Trafford.
[HIGGS *exits.* TRAFFORD *is left with
the sword in his hand limply at his
side. He throws the sword to the floor
in a fury of disgust. He goes to wings.
He pulls the desk and a stretcher on
stage. He sits at the desk and tries to
write. He abandons the attempt and
tears off his costume.*]
TRAFFORD: What's the use!
[*In neck-to-knee underwear he throws
himself down on the stretcher.
Blackout.*]

SCENE EIGHT

Darkness. A lamp beam appears. It moves across the stage. It comes to rest on TRAFFORD *asleep on his stretcher. It moves away to the desk. It shines on the papers. A red-gloved hand collects up the papers from the desk. The lamp beam moves across the stage and stops. The papers are thrown down. The lamp is put on the ground. The red-gloved hands screw up some of the papers. Then a match is lit. The papers begin to burn.* TRAFFORD *is dimly lit up. He wakes, sniffs, reacts and rushes towards the fire. The lamp is hastily picked up.* TRAFFORD *grabs the figure by the arm and grapples with it briefly. The figure escapes.* TRAFFORD *stamps out the fire. He turns on the light. He has a red glove in his hand. Blackout.]*

SCENE NINE

The stage, next day. TRAFFORD *is at his desk trying to write. The arrival of two enthusiastic* CHEMISTS *has coincided with a visit by the* NEWSPAPER MAGNATE. *The* CHEMISTS *are giving a demonstration of a moving picture projector. Its beam is aimed out at the audience.*

MAGNATE: Ah. The world of the cinematographe. A world of magic. Of life drawn real and wriggling from a conjuror's hat.

TRAFFORD: [*writing furiously, not watching*] I'm watching.

FIRST CHEMIST: The process is quite simple. One hundred grams of silver nitrate . . .

SECOND CHEMIST: . . . $AgNO_3$ . . .

FIRST CHEMIST: . . . soluble in fifty drops of distilled water . . .

TRAFFORD: [*not listening*] I'm listening.

MAGNATE: A world of miracles. Of Lazarus rising and rising again at eight p.m. every night of the week. Think of the takings.

TRAFFORD: [*signalling for quiet*] I'm thinking. I'm thinking.

FIRST CHEMIST: Sodium hyposulphite . . .

SECOND CHEMIST: . . . Hypo . . .

FIRST CHEMIST: . . . soluble in boiling water . . .

SECOND CHEMIST: . . . one part to two . . .

FIRST CHEMIST: . . . insoluble in alcohol, of course . . .

SECOND CHEMIST: . . . of course . . .

TRAFFORD: Of course!

[*He scribbles.*]

MAGNATE: Of course, all the world's a stage to the film-maker. There life spills before him unadulterated, unscripted, unhampered by wires and pulleys and canvas . . .

TRAFFORD: What's that you say?

FIRST CHEMIST: We work with two fixing baths . . .

SECOND CHEMIST: . . . ten minutes for the neg. in the first bath . . .

FIRST CHEMIST: . . . five in the second bath . . .

TRAFFORD: Second-class entertainment.

MAGNATE: I'm investing my money in the cinematographe. Spencer, Longford, the Taits, J. C. Williamson. They're all getting into it. There's a boom coming.

TRAFFORD: They jerk, they flicker. They're scratchy, they break.

MAGNATE: [*picking up the film cans and reading off the titles*] Look at these. *Busy Day at the Homebush Abattoir, Breakers at the Bogey Hole, The Gallop Past of the Sydney Fire*

Brigade, Rush Hour at Redfern.
Marvellous.

TRAFFORD: The subjects scamper about
as if they had ants in their pants.

MAGNATE: Already the most patronised
of all public entertainments. On the
moving screen you get all the vital
reality, and you are spared the
boredom of hearing the oft-times
indifferent actors' talk.

TRAFFORD: It's not natural. It's the deaf
man's view of the world. All action
and no talk.

FIRST CHEMIST: Kodak are working on
a new celluloid . . .

SECOND CHEMIST: Perfectly safe.

FIRST CHEMIST: Doesn't explode.

SECOND CHEMIST: Available soon.

FIRST CHEMIST: One day there'll be
talkies.

MAGNATE: The sky's the limit. Earth-
quakes, horseraces, snowstorms—

TRAFFORD: We do them.

MAGNATE: —railway disasters, cricket
matches—

TRAFFORD: We do them all on stage.

MAGNATE: —ships colliding, chimneys
demolished—

TRAFFORD: Easy.

MAGNATE: —and rebuilt a moment
later? Cars driving up walls. Angels
flying through clouds—

TRAFFORD: Cheap tricks with light.
That's all it is. Gazing on shadows.
Mere illusions.

FIRST CHEMIST: Slow motion.

SECOND CHEMIST: Reverse wind.

FIRST CHEMIST: Double exposure.

TRAFFORD: Fake. It's all fake.

MAGNATE: It's a goldmine. The
theatre's finished. J.C.'s made fifty
thousand pounds in eighteen months.

There's four and a half million
people in Australia. You can show
the same film at the same time all
over the country.

FIRST CHEMIST: Multiple copies.

SECOND CHEMIST: Distribution.

MAGNATE: And for features all you
need are fifty horses, a few roughriders, a bagful of guns, all your
aunts and uncles for the crowd
scenes—and, of course, a pretty girl
given plenty of exposure. Let them
loose in the bush down at Brookvale
for a few days—and you've got it.
Enough to appeal to crowded houses
six nights a week.

TRAFFORD: Live theatre's got a great
future, Frank.

MAGNATE: You move too slowly,
George. The twentieth century'll wipe
you away.

TRAFFORD: I'm working on a new play
right now. A twentieth century play.
All about aviation. The fascination of
flight! We're about to soar into the
twentieth century, Frank. The
Empire's about to sprout wings!

MAGNATE: Oh. Well . . . that's what
I came down to talk to you about.

TRAFFORD: You did?

MAGNATE: I'm withdrawing my backing
from the Empire Theatre.

TRAFFORD: You're what?

MAGNATE: I've put all my dough into
films. Every last penny. There's a
boom coming, George. I'm going to
be rich.

[*Blackout.*]

SCENE TEN

TRAFFORD, *in neck-to-knee underwear,
stands alone beside his desk. Australian
bush props are stacked around. The bi-*

plane hangs above. TRAFFORD's *movements are somewhat wooden and puppet-like. He looks up uncomfortably at the bi-plane. He looks down at his desk overflowing with papers. He moves the desk. Its scraping hurts his head. He fumbles in the desk drawer and brings out an egg. He puts the egg on the desk. Then in the drawer he finds a champagne glass. He knocks the egg on the side of the desk and breaks it into the glass. He searches in the drawer again. He brings out a small milk jug and pours milk into the glass over the egg. He comes forward and raises the glass in a toast.*

TRAFFORD: To this—

[*Pause.*]

womb.

[*He goes to drink. The sight of the egg upsets him. He attempts to break the yolk by stirring with his finger. It won't break. He proposes the toast again.*]

To this—

[*Pause.*]

wide world.

[*He goes to drink but can't manage it. He puts the glass down on the desk. He fumbles in the drawer and brings out a skipping rope. He looks uneasily at the bi-plane overhead. He skips but has to stop. From the drawer he takes a jock strap. He puts it on, then skips again, doing peppers.*]

Heal-thy bo-dy,
Heal-thy mind.
Heal-thy bo-dy,
Heal-thy . . .

[*He can't go on. He drops the rope and holds his head and chest. He gasps.*]

That feels better.

[*He gets the glass and raises it towards the bi-plane.*]

To the splendour of the vision.

[*He drinks, winces, then crosses himself.*]

Fuel to the fire. Nothing like a raw egg to get the imagination going.

[*He tosses the glass over his shoulder.*]

Now to work.

[*He picks up a playscript from the desk and takes it to the stretcher where his clothes are. He begins dressing in an aviator's outfit. He consults the playscript as he dresses.*]

Thus the worm spins. Puts its armour on. Wraps its wriggle in darkness. Prepares itself for flight.

[*He does up the buttons.*]

Thus in its cave it dreams. Cocooned, it contemplates clouds. Suffocating, it fashions wings, it analyses air.

[*He puts on a pair of elastic-sided boots.*]

Fearful of the distant ground, it reaches out sure-footed legs.

[*He puts on a leather flying cap with goggles.*]

Out of blindness it grows eyes. Out of groping, an articulate head.

[*He puts on a harness.*]

Mindful of the thinness of wings, the necessary thinness, it fixes its form. Sensing the battering air, it tautens.

[*He takes a pillow from the stretcher. Using a large belt he ties it to his front.*]

Trembling, the worm considers his prospects. His cocoon is warm, is strangling. His wings are rainbow glossy, thin as razors. Gleaming, his nightmare eye seeks light.

[HIGGS *and* STAGEHANDS *enter.* HIGGS *holds the end of a fly wire.*]

HIGGS: Everything's ready.

TRAFFORD: We are about to take the world flying, Higgs.

[*During the following dialogue between* TRAFFORD *and* ESSON, HIGGS *supervises the lowering of the bi-plane to the floor, tests its wires, then ties another pillow to* TRAFFORD's *back using the skipping rope which he picks up from the floor.* HIGGS *tests the plane and its wires thoroughly. Enter* ESSON.]

ESSON: Mr Trafford?

TRAFFORD: Oh, yes. Mr Esson. You've come at a bad time.

ESSON: You did say Monday.

TRAFFORD: This is the theatre, Esson. Plans change from day to day.

ESSON: You've read my play?

TRAFFORD: I'm working on a new play myself. A man breaks free of his stifling past and soars aloft into a world of creative freedom. What do you think of it?

ESSON: Very symbolic.

TRAFFORD: Oh. That's unfortunate. Audiences don't like symbolism: they think they'll catch something from it. Treat it like the plague, they do.

ESSON: What the Australian theatre-goer needs is a boot in the bum.

TRAFFORD: Don't you dare attack the theatregoer's bum. We need it too badly. There are twenty thousand three hundred seats in this city's theatres. We need lots of bums.

ESSON: They only come to the theatre to blow raspberries.

TRAFFORD: You're an intellectual, Esson. Intellectualism is not a popular Australian sport.

ESSON: Ah. If only I were the Victor Trumper of verse. Do you know how difficult it is for poets in this country? There are only two words to rhyme with Australia: 'failure' and 'genitalia'.

[TRAFFORD *pauses and thinks a moment.*]

TRAFFORD: What about 'dahlia'?

ESSON: Not nearly so useful.

TRAFFORD: But more publishable. Free of the ugly rearing monsters sex and intellectualism.

ESSON: How is it you play Shakespeare, then?

TRAFFORD: Australians like to come and gawk at Shakespeare occasionally. In his cage.

ESSON: Like some freak.

TRAFFORD: Like some wild animal. We keep him locked up in the theatre. Where he belongs. We couldn't have him roaming the streets. 'Intelligence At Large' the papers would cry.

ESSON: I do believe you *have* read my play.

TRAFFORD: Don't get excited. I'm not going to use it.

ESSON: But you agree, don't you? We need a national, intelligent drama. Something beyond bushrangers and convicts. We need a theatre that'll break free from its stifling past.

TRAFFORD: Start it yourself. Good luck.

ESSON: But it won't work.

TRAFFORD: Then we agree on one thing.

ESSON: It won't work until Australians rouse themselves from their heroic wet dreams. Until the workers stop worshipping the great god Commerce. Until the newspapers do more than just wrap up the political and sporting rubbish. Until the church stops slaughtering innocence, the pubs are burned down, the factories turned over, and parliament fumigated. Not until the suburban home has been exorcised of its devils: Dullness and Security, will there be hope for a drama which soars on wings of Dionysean adventure. Australians are too docile to fly, Mr Trafford. They're too moral, too satisfied, too passionless. They're cattle grazing on suburban lawns, producing only the milk of mindless mediocrity. How could those cows jump for the moon?

[*Pause.*]

TRAFFORD: I am impressed.

ESSON: I'm sorry, sir. Sometimes I get carried away.

TRAFFORD: What do you think, Higgs? Have we here a budding leader for the revolution of the masses?

HIGGS: It sounds like pretty dangerous stuff to me, sir.

ESSON: Exactly. Danger is what we need. Healthy danger.

TRAFFORD: Well. Stay and watch my maiden flight, then.

[STAGEHANDS *take hold of the fly wires:* FIRST *and* SECOND STAGEHANDS *control the ascent wire at left;* HIGGS *the tracking wire at right.*]

HIGGS: All set, I think.

TRAFFORD: Just be gentle, will you.

[ROSIE *enters.*]

Ah, Rosie. We need a nurse standing by. Won't you oblige?

ROSIE: [*barring his entry to the plane*] Let someone else do this. Why not one of the roughriders?

TRAFFORD: [*moving her aside and entering the plane*] There's nothing to worry about. [*Patting the side of the plane*] I'm christening her the 'Muse

of Fire'. Haul away, Higgs! Let's ascend that brightest heaven of invention!

[*The* STAGEHANDS *pull on the wire. With a sudden gut-wrenching sweep,* TRAFFORD's *plane goes up much too fast. It swings wildly.* HIGGS *tries to control it with the tracking wire.* TRAFFORD *continues heroically.*]

TRAFFORD: 'A kingdom for a stage, princes to act, and monarchs to behold the swelling scene!' God. What a view! The city sprawls down there, its sweaty suburbs aching outwards. All along the writhing shoreline, the sea and land caress. The paddocks stretch like long green fingers towards the sensual swell of the mountains— Hey!

[*The plane jerks downwards a little. The* STAGEHANDS *struggle with the wires. The plane plummets downwards frighteningly.*]

Aaaargh!

[*The* STAGEHANDS *haul on the wires. The plane steadies.* HIGGS *manipulates his wire and orders the* STAGEHANDS *to do similarly.*]

HIGGS: I think we've got it under control now, sir.

ROSIE: Let him down.

HIGGS: Do you want another try?

ROSIE: Don't you dare!

TRAFFORD: Yes, Higgs. I'm ready.

[*The* STAGEHANDS *pull and the plane shoots back up.* HIGGS *works the tracking wire. The plane flies slowly across the stage.*]

Ah. Now we climb above the mountains. We cross the rolling plains. We track above the trackless waste. We spy in the distance the great mirage, the inland sea . . .

[*As he speaks the plane disappears

BEHIND MUSE OF FIRE by Nigel Krauth

It was a difficult business deciding on my major themes when the STC commissioned me to write a play last year. But it was eventually the Playhouse Theatre itself which made the best suggestions.

Muse of Fire is set in 1910. It concerns the beginnings of the film industry in Australia, and the shock-waves sent through the live theatre industry by the advent of film.

The first boom in film-making (there were more than forty major movies released in 1911 alone) coincided with the first flights by motor-driven aircraft over the nation's cities.

In 1910 there was an urgent sense of the twentieth-century's arrival. Together the aviation and film industries gave a severe shake-up to the old laws of gravity, time, place and perspective.

In 1910 the modern spirit was breaking free, entering new dimensions. The man in the street was about to be swept off his feet by the most exciting of modern technologies.

In *Muse of Fire* George Trafford is an old-style theatre owner/manager/actor. His ailing theatre, The Empire, struggles on while all around is the bustle and promise of the rush into films, and the reckless romantic heroism of early aviation.

Nothing ever goes smoothly for Trafford. His acting troupe is unreliable, his stage-hands are exceedingly rebellious, his separated wife still demands to be the leading lady, and he is plagued by a young playwright—Louis Esson—who insists that he is the future hope of Australian drama. In addition, there is somebody trying to burn down the theatre.

The one person who sticks by Trafford through thick and thin is his mistress Rosie Bellowes. She remains faithful to him in spite of his obsessive visions, his hopeless depressions, his outrageous ecstasies, and his ridiculous cowardice. She remains faithful to the germ of genius buried deep within him, the aspect of himself she tries desperately to lead him to.

Central to Trafford's problems is the fact that live theatre has for decades mounted the most spectacular productions—from blizzards to chariot races, from ships colliding at sea to massed armies on elephant-back. Who needed film? Late nineteeth-century live theatre was rich, lively, spectacular, expensive—and three-dimensional.

Yet patrons flocked to see the jerky, flickering, silent celluloid images. And the kind of show movie-goers best loved was that in which they were themselves depicted. The most popular movies up to 1910 were street-scene documentaries: "Marvellous Melbourne", "The Royal Easter Show", "The Gallop Past of the Sydney Fire Brigade", and so on.

There were less than a dozen feature films made prior to 1910. But things were about to change. More than eighty features were made in the three years following. Some of Australia's live theatre managers, like J.C. Williamson, made fortunes by turning their interests to film. All this at a time when Hollywood was a patch of scrub and sandy bush tracks!

In spite of being set seventy-five years ago, *Muse of Fire* is a play concerned with modern themes. It is about twentieth-century love, twentieth-century technology and politics, twentieth-century imagination and heroism. I don't detect much to suggest we are now greatly wiser in these areas than we were seventy-five years ago.

To look at 1910 is to look at some of the roots of present-day problems plaguing industrial and gender relations, theatre arts and technology. Since 1910 we have fallen from the same heights over and over. And have picked ourselves up again each time.

Muse of Fire has songs, dance, tableaux, vignettes, silent movies, an aeroplane which flies, a bit of Shakespeare, a bit of Esson, a bit of melodrama, a naughty bit, a couple of jokes even I find funny, a *soupcon* of subtle symbolism, poetic speeches, moving declamations, a raw egg in milk, gutsy dialogue, miraculous costume changes, astounding scenery, brilliant cast, superb direction. And the theatre burns down.

I can't wait to see it.

NIGEL KRAUTH Playwright

Nigel Krauth was born in Sydney in 1949. He studied literature at universities in Newcastle, Canberra and Brisbane. After eight years as an academic, he turned to full-time writing, and published his best-seller novel *Matilda, My Darling*. It was a joint winner of the Australian/Vogel Literary Award in 1982. Nigel has published short stories, had radio plays broadcast overseas, and was an editor of Inprint Magazine. In 1981 he received a New Writers Fellowship from the Literature Board of the Australia Council, and in 1984, a Writers Fellowship to work on a second novel. *Muse of Fire*, Nigel's first stage play, has been commissioned by the State Theatre Company with assistance from the Literature Board of the Australia Council.

KEITH GALLASCH Director

Keith Gallasch is the Artistic Director of the State Theatre Company. Born and educated in Adelaide, he has been a teacher, academic and the co-founder of Troupe Theatre. While with Troupe, Keith worked as an actor, writer and director and also appeared in Stephen Wallace's feature film *Stir*. In recent years he has written three plays for youth theatre companies in Adelaide and Canberra. He has been Chairperson of the Association of Community Theatres, a member of the South Australian Governments' Arts Grants Advisory Committee and is currently a member of the Adelaide Writers' Week Committee and of the Literature Board of the Australia Council. He was also film reviewer for ABC radio (Adelaide) for over two years. Keith Gallasch was appointed Artistic Director of the State Theatre Company in 1983 and was responsible for programming the astoundingly successful 1984 season.

COLIN MITCHELL Designer

Colin Mitchell, the resident designer for Magpie Theatre (the State Theatre Company's theatre for young people) has designed *Muse of Fire*. A graduate of the Preston Institute of Technology in Melbourne, Colin's designs include *Stalin—The Musical* for Footbridge Theatre, *The Relapse* for Cell Block Theatre and *The Rocky Horror Show* for The Riverina Trucking Company. Since moving to Adelaide and Magpie Theatre, his work includes designing *The Expedition, Animal Acts, Teen-Ages* and *Definitely Not The Last. Muse of Fire* is his first design for the State Theatre Company's main stage.

JOHN COMEADOW Lighting Designer

John Comeadow has spent fifteen years in professional theatre and his recent designs have been for Nimrod Theatre, Sydney Theatre Company and the State Theatre Company of South Australia. In 1984 he was awarded a designer's development grant from the Australia Council Theatre Board, during which he designed *Gentlemen Prefer Blondes* and *Key Largo* for the New Moon Theatre Company. He has also designed for Human Veins Dance Theatre, Australian Dance Theatre, Dance Works of Melbourne and Magpie Theatre's Melbourne season of *No Worries*. For the State Theatre Company in 1984, John lit Esson's *The Time Is Not Yet Ripe* and Patrick White's *The Season at Sarsaparilla*. He is currently the resident lighting designer for the State Theatre Company.

IAN FARR Musical Director

Born in South Australia, Ian Farr trained at the Sydney Conservatorium of Music. He has worked as a classical musician with the Sydney Symphony Orchestra and a music programmer with the ABC. Ian has been a prolific composer for theatre, radio, cabaret and dance. He has worked with singers such as Margaret Roadnight, Jeannie Lewis and Mary Haire. State Theatre Company productions for which he has composed and/or performed include *Royal Show, The Marriage of Figaro, Pal Joey, Romeo and Juliet* and *The Conquest of Carmen Miranda*.

THE PLAYREADING ADVISORY PANEL

The Playreading Advisory Panel was formed in 1976 to encourage Australian playwriting. As a free service for aspiring playwrights, the panel provides helpful criticism and selects several plays every year for a directed reading by the Company. For further information contact Rose Wilson on 51 5151.

THE PERFORMING ARTS COLLECTION OF SOUTH AUSTRALIA

Includes a wealth of fascinating performing arts memorabilia from the fields of opera, dance, drama, variety, music, radio and circus which is available to the public and provides a major resource collection for students of performing arts. People interested in seeing the memorabilia on display or donating performing arts material can phone 42 8332 during normal office hours or visit 79 Beulah Road, Norwood SA 5067.

The State Theatre Company of South Australia
Adelaide Festival Centre
King William Road
ADELAIDE SA 5000
Telephone: (08) 51 5151

OUR THANKS TO

WHEN YOU DESERVE THE BEST . . .

MINCHINBURY CHAMPAGNE

Ansett

Bev Freeman uses KERASTASE and L'ORÉAL OF PARIS

**SOUTH AUSTRALIAN FILM
CORPORATION
SOUND DEPARTMENT**

CHARACTERS

GEORGE TRAFFORD: a theatre owner and manager
ROSIE BELLOWES: an actress, his mistress
MOLLY TRAFFORD: separated from him, ex-leading lady
ELTON HIGGS: stagehands' union leader
LOUIS ESSON: playwright

AVIATOR	STAGEHAND 1
CHEMIST 1	STAGEHAND 2
CHEMIST 2	WORKER
CONTRACTOR	YOUNG ACTOR
INSURANCE ASSESSOR	
MAYOR	ACTRESS 3
NEWSPAPER MAGNATE	CARETAKER WOMAN
OLD ACTOR	MUSIC PLUGGER
PLAYER PILOT	NEWSGIRL
POLICEMAN	OLD ACTRESS
PRIVATE INVESTIGATOR	SEAMSTRESS
REPORTER	YOUNG ACTRESS
	PHOTOGRAPHER
ACCOMPANIST	

This play is set on the premises of the Empire Theatre, Pitt Street, Sydney, in 1910. The set comprises a proscenium arch with the wings on either side exposed.

The characters and events in this play are entirely imaginary and bear no relation to any real person or actual happening.

Muse of Fire

by Nigel Krauth

CAST

GEORGE TRAFFORD	Douglas Hedge
ROSIE BELLOWES	Natalie Bate
MOLLY TRAFFORD	Deborah Kennedy
LOUIS ESSON, PLAYER AVIATOR	Andrew Tighe
ELTON HIGGS	Peter Finlay
SOLICITOR, MAYOR, REPORTER, STAGEHAND 2, CHEMIST 2	Ross Williams
PRIVATE INVESTIGATOR, STAGEHAND 1, CHEMIST 1, NEWSBOY, PHOTOGRAPHER	William Zappa
INSURANCE ASSESSOR, AVIATOR, WORKER, YOUNG ACTOR	Terry Crawford
NEWSPAPER MAGNATE, OLD ACTOR, CONTRACTOR, POLICEMAN	David Kendall
CARETAKER WOMAN, ACTRESS 3	Joan Murray
OLD ACTRESS	Dina Panozzo
YOUNG ACTRESS, SEAMSTRESS	Morna Seres
MUSIC PLUGGER, THEATRE PIANIST	Ian Farr (Musical Director)

NB. George, Rosie and the four actors play various roles in *Henry V*, The Bushranger Melodrama and *The Time Is Not Yet Ripe*.

This production opened at the Playhouse, Festival Centre, Adelaide, on August 2, 1985.

DIRECTOR	Keith Gallasch
DESIGNER	Colin Mitchell
LIGHTING DESIGNER	John Comeadow
MUSICAL DIRECTOR	Ian Farr
STAGE MANAGER	Shauna Roche
ASSISTANT STAGE MANAGER	Jenny Enilane
HEAD MECHANIST	Martin Smith
MECHANISTS	Greg O'Reilly
	Geoff Munn
	Gary Coats
HEAD ELECTRICIAN	Chris Luscombe
LIGHTING OPERATOR	Rosie Moroney
SOUND	Stuart Kirby
DRESSERS	Sylvia Horsman
	Zita Weelius
HAIRDRESSER	Bev Freeman
VOICE TEACHER	Bill Bamford
MOVEMENT	John Nobbs

The State Theatre Company gratefully acknowledges the assistance of the Government of South Australia and the Theatre, Music and Literature Boards of the Australia Council, the Federal Government's arts funding and advisory body.

AUTHOR'S ACKNOWLEDGEMENTS

This play was commissioned by the State Theatre Company of South Australia.

For assistance in the writing of this play I make grateful acknowledgement to the State Theatre Company of South Australia and the Literature Board of the Australia Council.

I also ackowledge the creative and critical assistance of Keith Gallasch, Caron Krauth, Colin Mitchell, and members of the Adelaide cast and company.

NATALIE BATE

Natalie Bate graduated from NIDA in 1973 and has since worked for the major professional theatre companies and in theatre-in-education. She played lead roles in many classical productions for the Melbourne Theatre Company and performed *The Soldier's Tale* through mime, dance and recitation as a one-woman show in the Seymour Centre. In 1981 Natalie won the Sydney Critics' Circle Award for Best Actress for her interpretation of the title role in *Mary Barnes: A Journey Through Madness*. She has done extensive television work and appeared in the films *Mad Dog Morgan, Dimboola, Tread Softly* and *Desire*. The two years prior to joining the State Theatre Company she spent living and working in Europe. She spends as much time as possible painting and doing movement and yoga classes.

TERENCE CRAWFORD

Terence Crawford is one of the two new NIDA graduates to join the company this year. Before attending NIDA Terence had a year's professional experience with the Hunter Valley Theatre Company appearing in such productions as *Treasure Island, No Names . . . No Packdrill* and John O'Donohue's *Essington Lewis: I Am Work*.

PETER FINLAY

Peter Finlay began performing professionally in 1975 and three years later joined the Victorian College of the Arts. After his graduation in 1981 he co-founded Theatre Works for which, among other things, he wrote and directed *The Middle of the Road Show*. Other productions in which he has appeared are *Storming Mont Albert By Tram* (performed on the No.42 tram), *The Tempest, The White Hotel* and *The Cherry Orchard*. He has been in many television series and in the film *Mouth to Mouth;* most recently in *Anzacs,* due for release this year.

DOUGLAS HEDGE

Originally from Sydney, Douglas Hedge worked for over seven years with the Queensland Theatre Company in productions including *Old Times, Summer of the Seventeenth Doll* and *The Removalists*. He subsequently joined the Melbourne Theatre Company appearing in many productions including *Hobsons Choice, In Celebration* and Clem Gorman's adaptation of A.B. Facey's *A Fortunate Life* at the Victorian Arts Centre. Douglas's television credits include *The Keepers, Prisoner* and *Special Squad*.

DAVID KENDALL

A graduate of the University of Melbourne, David Kendall was a founding member of the La Mama Company (later the Australian Performing Group) and performed in and/or directed many of the earliest plays of Jack Hibberd and John Romeril. He then studied for two years at the Drama Centre, London, before returning to Australia as Director of University Theatre at Melbourne University. His many performances include Kurt in *Dance of Death*, Leo Sewell in *Bleedin' Butterflies*, Estragon in *Waiting For Godot*, Ulysses and Thersites in *Troilus and Cressida*. He has also appeared in all major television series and recently in the film *Strikebound*. In Adelaide he appeared in *Accidental Death of an Anarchist* and directed Henry Salter's play *The Case*. He left the staff of the Flinders Drama Centre to join the State Theatre Company in 1985.

DEBORAH KENNEDY

Deborah Kennedy's career began with five years of touring with Pageant Theatre-in-Education. In 1975 she joined the Nimrod Acting School and subsequently appeared in such productions as *Much Ado About Nothing* (which toured to Adelaide), *Travelling North* and *Accidental Death of an Anarchist*. She has also worked for the Sydney Theatre and New Moon Theatre Companies. Deborah Kennedy has previously appeared with the State Theatre Company in *The Revenger's Tragedy* and *No End of Blame*. She has done a great deal of television work including *Restless Years* and *1915* and is soon to be featured in *A Country Practice*. Her film work includes the award-winning *Temperament Unsuited, Tim* and *I Can't Get Started*.

JOAN MURRAY

Joan Murray has worked with various mainstage, theatre-in-education and community companies. Her most recent work has been with the Theatre A.C.T. and included *On Our Selection, Cloud Nine, Mother Courage, The Perfectionist* and *Female Parts*. While in Canberra, Joan also directed and worked with a dance company and compiled and performed a one-woman play about Dame Mary Gilmore.

DINA PANOZZO

Dina Panozzo is an Adelaide actor who studied at the Victorian College of the Arts until 1982. Since graduation she has appeared in *Tales From Land Shut* for the Pram Factory, *Don't Stand on Ceremony* for St Martin's Theatre, *Exploring Shakespeare* for the Melbourne Theatre Company, *The Time of Your Life* at the Comedy Cafe and *Il Magnifico* for Nimrod. Dina has worked in both film and television and her TV credits include *City West* (for 0-28), *Carson's Law* and *A Country Practice*.

MORNA SERES

Morna Seres graduated from NIDA in 1984 and her appointment to the State Theatre Company is her first professional engagement. While studying, Morna appeared in many NIDA productions including *Ivanov* which was directed by the State Theatre Company's current Associate Director Peter King.

ANDREW TIGHE

Andrew Tighe first performed with the Sydney University Drama Society (SUDS) in productions which included *Gimme Shelter, Bartholomew Fair* and *The Real Inspector Hound*. He then joined the Sydney Theatre Company and played in such productions as *Nicholas Nickleby, Hamlet* and *Cyrano De Bergerac*. Last year he appeared in the highly successful State Theatre Company production of *Private Lives*. His television credits include *Young Doctors, A Country Practice* and *Special Squad*.

ROSS WILLIAMS

Ross Williams began his acting career in 1974 working for the Melbourne Theatre Company's theatre-in-education team. He worked professionally in New Zealand before attending the Victorian College of the Arts in 1978. Since his graduation in 1980, he has worked with many companies in such productions as *I Can Give You a Good Time* for the Playbox (which toured successfully to the Sydney Festival in 1984), *Back to Bourke Street* for the Last Laugh Theatre Restaurant, *Cheapside* and *A Midsummer Night's Dream* for the Melbourne Theatre Company. His television credits include *Infinity Limited, The Keepers* and *The Sullivans*. His film appearances include *Squizzy* and *The Patsy*.

WILLIAM ZAPPA

William Zappa trained at the Central School of Speech and Drama in London and has been acting professionally since 1966. His theatre experience in Australia includes performing in *Bertolt Brecht Leaves L.A.* and *Fool For Love* for Playbox, *Long Days' Journey into Night* for St Martin's Theatre and *Translations* for the Melbourne Theatre Company. He has appeared in all of the major television series and in the films *Mad Max 2, Secret Discovery of Australia* and *Women of the Sun* for which he won the Penguin Award for Best Actor. During the 1984 Adelaide Festival, William Zappa was much applauded for his interpretation of the title role in the State Theatre Company's production of Molière's play *Don Juan*.

high into the fly tower. HIGGS *and the* STAGEHANDS *continue at the wires.* ROSIE *and* ESSON *follow* TRAFFORD's *progress high up. Suddenly the tension in the* STAGEHANDS' *wire gives and there is a corresponding sickening crash as the plane, canvases, and* TRAFFORD *plummet to the floor.* ROSIE *and* ESSON *run to the heap of wreckage.* HIGGS *and the* STAGEHANDS *join them, urgently sifting through the debris.*]

ROSIE: [*screaming*] Where is he?

ESSON: Mr Trafford? Are you all right?

[HIGGS *and the* STAGEHANDS *throw aside identifiable pieces of plane wreckage. They lift off a broken wing then stop, startled.* ROSIE *screams and dives on* TRAFFORD's *inert body.*]

ROSIE: George!

[ROSIE *and* ESSON *raise a dazed* TRAFFORD *to this feet.* HIGGS *and the* STAGEHANDS *assist. They relieve him of his pillows.* ROSIE *screams at* HIGGS.]

It was your fault.

HIGGS: Was not. The tackle failed.

TRAFFORD: [*trying to shake off the helpers; weakly*] Let me alone.

ROSIE: [*screaming*] Why didn't you check it?

HIGGS: I did check it.

ROSIE: [*hysterical*] It's an assassination attempt.

HIGGS: Shut up, will you!

TRAFFORD: [*painfully standing on his own*] OK. Forget it.

ROSIE: He tried to murder you.

HIGGS: Jesus Christ. It was an accident.

TRAFFORD: [*painfully*] I said forget it.

[*He tests his limbs.*]

There's no harm done . . . I don't think. I'm fine.

[*He tests his limbs again.*]

Good as gold. See?

[*Pause.*]

When can we try again?

ROSIE: [*icily threatening*] Don't you dare!

ESSON: I hardly think that's wise.

TRAFFORD: Only joking. Only joking. As a first flight it was—an abortion. But I was *up*, wasn't I? I think that's cause enough for a celebration.

ESSON: You mean we need a drink. I couldn't agree more.

[TRAFFORD *takes* ESSON *by the arm. He takes a step and staggers.* ESSON *holds him up. He limps noticeably as they walk. The* CARETAKER WOMAN *enters and begins sweeping up wreckage.*]

ROSIE: Bloody men. Being heroes.

TRAFFORD: I'll fly yet, my love. You'll see.

[*They all exit angrily, except for the* CARETAKER WOMAN. *She is left sweeping.*]

[*Blackout.*]

INTERVAL

SCENE ONE

The stage. It is interval. STAGEHANDS *are moving props, setting them up for a hold-up scene of a bushranger melodrama.* TRAFFORD *is in the wings, left, dressed as Captain Thunderbolt. The* SECOND STAGEHAND *holds the curtain rope.*

TRAFFORD: [*consulting his watch and peering out at the house*] Many abandoned us during the interval?

SECOND STAGEHAND: [*peering out*] Only the drunkards. Still in the bar, I suppose.

TRAFFORD: Give them an extra minute.

[*In the wings right, the* ACTING TROUPE *waits in colonial costume.* ROSIE *is dressed as a squatter's daughter.* HIGGS *deals with the props.*]

HIGGS: It *was* an accident, Trafford falling this afternoon. The pulley was broken.

ROSIE: Don't you dare talk to us.

HIGGS: [*grabbing her arm*] It was his own fault. He's too stingy to replace the old equipment.

ROSIE: Let me go!

HIGGS: I don't like being accused of underhand tactics. That's not my idea of unionism.

[ROSIE *breaks free.* TRAFFORD *signals. The* ACTING TROUPE *moves on stage.*]

TRAFFORD: We can't wait any longer, Joe. Give us the curtain.

[TRAFFORD *draws a pistol and moves boldly on stage.*]

Bail up! Bail up!

[*Blackout.*]

SCENE TWO

The wings left. The bushranger melodrama has progressed. ACTRESSES, *including* ROSIE, *stand waiting in costume. They peer off where shouting can be heard: 'There they are. Follow them'.* TRAFFORD *runs on from stage with the* OLD ACTOR *in bushranger costume.*

OLD ACTOR: Where's Adrian?

TRAFFORD: Blast him.

OLD ACTOR: Shall I say he has the sandy blight?

TRAFFORD: I hardly think it'll convince.

[ESSON *enters.*]

Ah. Mr Esson. Get your coat off.

ESSON: I beg your pardon?

[*They relieve* ESSON *of his coat and bowler. They shove onto his head a bush hat and press a shotgun into his hand.*]

TRAFFORD: Welcome to Thunderbolt's gang. You're about to be shot.

[*They propel* ESSON *off right. He is protesting. Shouts are heard: 'There's one of them'. Then gun shots.* ESSON *is thrown back, minus the gun. The* OLD ACTOR *is laughing.*]

Excellent. Excellent.

ESSON: [*lying on the floor*] Jesus Christ.

TRAFFORD: [*peering off for his cue*] Don't complain, old man. This is the world of the theatre you're so keen to enter.

[TRAFFORD *and the* OLD ACTOR *exit right. There are shouts from off: 'There he is. That's Thunderbolt'. Gun shots.* MOLLY *enters from left in street clothes.* ESSON *picks himself up*

*and dusts off. He finds his shirt is
torn under the arm.*]

ESSON: I hope he's going to buy me a
new one.

MOLLY: Who?

ESSON: That maniac, Trafford.

[ESSON *exits left. More gun shots.
Cries of the* OLD ACTOR *in pain.*
TRAFFORD *and* OLD ACTOR *re-enter.
The* OLD ACTOR *limps and clutches
his leg. There is stage blood on his
trousers.*]

TRAFFORD: [*seeing* MOLLY] Oh no.

MOLLY: Ambushed you, have I?

VOICES OFF: Come on out, Thunderbolt.
We know you're in there.

TRAFFORD: Can't you leave me alone?

MOLLY: I need money, George.

VOICES OFF: It's no use, Thunderbolt.
We've got you surrounded.

MOLLY: You owe me a lot, you know.

TRAFFORD: You must be joking.
[*Shouting off as Thunderbolt*] Don't
come any closer. I shall kill all of you!

VOICES OFF: Don't be a fool,
Thunderbolt. Give yourself up.

MOLLY: Half of what you have is mine.
I want you to hand it over.

TRAFFORD: Get out of here. You're
trespassing.

MOLLY: You've already used that line.

VOICES OFF: Come out with your hands
in the air.

TRAFFORD: [*as Thunderbolt*] All right.
Here I come.

[TRAFFORD *rushes out, firing his gun.
There is a terrific volley of gunfire.*
TRAFFORD *re-enters, clutching his
chest. A great splash of stage blood
stains his front and face.*]

MOLLY: [*indicating the stage blood*]
Oh my. That does suit you. Just your
colour, I think.

TRAFFORD: [*to* ROSIE, *trying to ignore*
MOLLY] You're on, love.

[ROSIE *moves on to the stage. There is
a piano introduction as* ROSIE *bows.*]

MOLLY: This used to be *my* song.

TRAFFORD: Quiet.

[*The song is sung briskly to the tune
of 'The Ryebuck Shearer'. The first
three lines of each verse are delivered
rough as guts while the last line is
sung in an exaggeratedly refined
manner.*]

ROSIE: From the time I was born I was
fed red meat,
Breakfast, lunch and dinner, and
some more for sweets,
Any plate piled with lamb, beef or
mutton I'd defeat;
I grew up as a squatter's daughter!

Chorus:
Come along, young men, what are
you waiting for?
I'm an eligible spinster, and a
whole lot more;
Let me grace your four-poster . . .
I hardly ever snore;
And of course I'm a squatter's
daughter!

From the time I was born I could
ride bareback,
I could rope a steer, I could whip a
black,
I could pick up a brown snake and
put it in a sack;
Thank the Lord I'm a squatter's
daughter!

Chorus

From the time I was born I could
earn my keep,
As busy as a blowie, I could wash,
sew and sweep,
I could turn my hand to anything . . .
[*tacet*] . . . haute cuisine or
crutching sheep;

Ain't that proof I'm a squatter's
  daughter?

Chorus

[*On the singing of the final chorus*
MOLLY *can hold herself back no
longer. She rushes on stage and joins
in the singing, claiming the song as
her own. She struts and stamps,
indicating that she probably sang the
song with even more rough verve than*
ROSIE. TRAFFORD, *finally unable to
control his rage, comes on stage. He
tries to grab* MOLLY. *He calls on the*
ACTING TROUPE *and* STAGEHANDS *for
assistance. There is booing and
hissing from the audience. As* MOLLY
is bundled off, TRAFFORD *turns to the
audience to apologise. An egg hits
him and splatters down his front. He
stands wide-eyed and speechless.
Blackout. The booing echoes and dies
away.*]

SCENE THREE

The stage. TRAFFORD *is on the
stretcher, his head propped up with
pillows.* ROSIE *sits beside him. She is
angry, he is depressed.*

TRAFFORD: I might as well give up.
  Instead of trying to fly on those wires
  I might as well hang myself with one.

ROSIE: Ever the King of Melodrama.

TRAFFORD: I'm not joking.

ROSIE: So that's what you think of life
  with me? You'd rather suicide.

TRAFFORD: Frank won't finance my
  play. The stagehands want a pound
  of my flesh. My wife's gone off the
  rails. Dear God. There's even somebody trying to burn the theatre down.

ROSIE: You didn't tell me that.

TRAFFORD: Oh, yes. A couple of nights
  back.

ROSIE: Who was it?

TRAFFORD: I didn't see the face. But
  I did get this.

  [*He produces the red glove.*]

ROSIE: A woman's.

TRAFFORD: Using my playscript for
  kindling.

ROSIE: [*taking the glove and putting it
  on*] Perfect fit.

  [*She begins caressing his face with the
  gloved hand.*]

TRAFFORD: [*avoiding the caress*] Take it
  off. It worries me. I certainly couldn't
  make love to you with that on.

ROSIE: [*still caressing*] I bet you could.

TRAFFORD: [*avoiding her*] I couldn't
  make love to you anyway. I'm
  deflated.

ROSIE: [*stopping caressing him*] Thanks
  a lot.

TRAFFORD: The bloody theatre
  finances! Frank's pulling out means
  we're on the skids.

ROSIE: [*fed up*] Go with him into
  films, then.

TRAFFORD: [*pleadingly*] Rosie!

ROSIE: Forget about flying with wires.
  Fly without wires.

TRAFFORD: It's impossible. I can't sell
  out on the theatre.

ROSIE: [*angrily*] You can't cut yourself
  free from the past . . . that's your
  problem. Don't you believe in your
  own vision?

TRAFFORD: Perhaps my vision's just a
  shot in the dark.

ROSIE: [*aggressively*] And what's the
  target?

TRAFFORD: Well . . . like I said . . . the
  new age . . . er . . . modern man's
  aspirations . . . heroism . . .

ROSIE: Maybe you'd do better to aim at yourself. Shoot inwards.

TRAFFORD: That sounds like suicide.

ROSIE: Maybe it does. [*Holding the glove in front of her between two fingers as if she might catch something nasty from it*] Tell me whose glove this is.

TRAFFORD: [*avoiding her*] How would I know?

ROSIE: I think you do.

TRAFFORD: Rosie, love. I have no proof.

ROSIE: Don't make me angry, George. [*Pause.*] Do you remember the first time you made love with me?

TRAFFORD: On the beach at Watson's Bay.

ROSIE: You threaded the maze of me. You made me say something I never intended to say to anyone.

TRAFFORD: You said: 'I love you'.

ROSIE: Do you remember what *you* said?

TRAFFORD: I'm not sure.

ROSIE: You said: 'I am new born'.

TRAFFORD: Did I?

ROSIE: Yes. You were lying. [*Blackout. Interscene in the wings. MOLLY and the SOLICITOR.*]

SOLICITOR: You're not following my instructions.

MOLLY: I need the stage. I need to embrace an audience. I need them to embrace me. I can't burn it down. I'm an actress, not an arsonist.

SOLICITOR: You'll end up with nothing. [*Blackout. The lights return to centre stage. ROSIE stands beside the stretcher. TRAFFORD is sitting on it.*]

ROSIE: Get the the police onto her.

TRAFFORD: I couldn't do that. She's still my wife.

ROSIE: Separated.

TRAFFORD: She's done no harm.

ROSIE: You can't have people dropping in whenever they want to, trying to burn the place down. Not even your wife.

TRAFFORD: How do you know it was her? It could have been anyone. Higgs and the stagehands. Even that young larrikin Esson. None of them bear me great affection.

ROSIE: Either you go to the police, or I go.

TRAFFORD: You go?

ROSIE: If you won't act in your own interests, I'll have to do it for you.

TRAFFORD: Look. I'll hire someone to keep an eye on her. I'll consult my solicitor. He can find me a private investigator. I'll discover exactly what she's up to. Is that good enough? [*Blackout. Interscene in the wings. The SOLICITOR sits at his office desk. He speaks into a telephone. Beside him, lounging arrogantly in a chair, is a nasty piece of work, the PRIVATE INVESTIGATOR.*]

SOLICITOR: Yes, Mr Trafford. I know just the man for the job. [*Pushing the INVESTIGATOR's feet from the desk*] As your solicitor, may I recommend Mr Splatt. Matrimonial cases are his specialty. [*The SOLICITOR indicates to the INVESTIGATOR to get himself ready.*] I'll contact him and bring him over. [*Blackout. The lights return to the centre stage. ROSIE and TRAFFORD stand on either side of the stretcher.*]

ROSIE: I am trying to help you. Can't you see your only hope is the film industry?

TRAFFORD: But my vision is of life, of

human spirits upraised, of largesse, of glory . . .

ROSIE: What's the difference between on stage and in film?

TRAFFORD: No. My vision breathes, transports, ascends. It lifts the god from within. Look down there! A street full of men all upstaring in amazement!

ROSIE: You've become the fool of your vision, George. The victim of it.

[*Pause.* TRAFFORD *sits on the stretcher and massages his brow.*]

TRAFFORD: Do you really think a film could catch all that?

ROSIE: Of course it could. They belong together, film and aviation. Whirring sprockets and wild imaginations.

TRAFFORD: But what happened to your love of theatre?

ROSIE: I gave it up. For you.

[*Pause.* TRAFFORD *holds his head in his hands.* ROSIE *sits beside him.*]

I'd give up many things for you. I believe that something golden is inside you.

TRAFFORD: You want to be midwife to my vision?

ROSIE: I want to bring your head out of the clouds.

[*Pause.*]

TRAFFORD: [*standing up, as if in revelation*] Of course! Why didn't I think of it before? A film about flying! The whole theatre will take off . . .

[*Blackout. Interscene in the wings. The* MAGNATE *turns off a movie projector and answers the phone. He is not pleased at being interrupted. While speaking he checks spools and the titles on reels of film in cans.*]

MAGNATE: Oh, George . . . What? . . .

A sensational idea, eh . . . What? . . . 'Camera in the Clouds'? . . . 'Eye in the Sky'? . . . What are you talking about, George? . . . I don't think you *could* attach a movie camera to the wings of a bi-plane. They're only made of canvas . . . Well, even so . . . Films cost a lot of money to make, George. A great deal of money . . . And you want to convert the Empire into a picture palace? . . .

[*He starts the projector rolling again.*]

Yes, I know I suggested it once . . . I'm very sorry, George. I'm fully committed.

[*He puts down the phone. Blackout. The lights return to the centre of the stage.* TRAFFORD *and* ROSIE *are under a blanket on the stretcher. She wears the red glove.*]

ROSIE: [*desperately*] I'm sorry.

TRAFFORD: It's not your fault.

ROSIE: [*gesturing with the glove*] I could strangle that Frank.

TRAFFORD: Steady on.

ROSIE: [*looking at the glove*] Only one thing for it, then.

TRAFFORD: What?

ROSIE: Fire.

TRAFFORD: What?

ROSIE: Burn the place down.

TRAFFORD: What?

ROSIE: Arson. [*Caressing him with her red-gloved hand*] Collect the insurance money. Start your own film company. Rebuild the theatre as a moving picture palace. *Voila!*

TRAFFORD: You are joking.

ROSIE: Do I look as though I'm joking?

TRAFFORD: It's a crazy idea.

ROSIE: All's crazy in love and war.

TRAFFORD: It's against the law.

ROSIE: Progress always is. Flying's against the law of gravity. Moving pictures go against all the laws of reality—time, place, perspective. Besides, there's an unwritten law that says old theatres always burn down.

TRAFFORD: But what you are suggesting is . . . enormous.

ROSIE: So is my love for you.

[*Pause.*]

TRAFFORD: [*seduced*] It's an intriguing idea. Get rid of this place. Build it up again. New company, new ideas. A whole new start. From the ashes of drama will rise the phoenix of films! By golly, why not! [*Ecstatically*] You're an inspiration, my love. I'll get in touch with the insurance people right away.

[TRAFFORD *begins to leave the stretcher.*]

ROSIE: [*pulling him back*] Hold on. There's plenty of time.

[*Enter an* INSURANCE ASSESSOR *in the wings. He is making a tour of inspection.* ROSIE *pulls* TRAFFORD *on top of herself.*]

TRAFFORD: [*happily*] Rosie, my love. What did I ever do to deserve you?

ROSIE: You inspired me to explore your possibilities.

[TRAFFORD *thrusts.*]

Ooh! Gently.

ASSESSOR: Ah, yes. Good ingress and egress. Wide vestibule. Fireproof stairway. No worries there.

[TRAFFORD *stops.*]

ROSIE: But you also frustrated the hell out of me.

TRAFFORD: Why?

ROSIE: By keeping me outside.

TRAFFORD: Never again, my love.

[TRAFFORD *thrusts.*]

ASSESSOR: Thick brick walls. Iron fire doors. Good use of non-combustible materials.

ROSIE: Ooh. A little more to the left. That's the spot.

[TRAFFORD *stops.*]

TRAFFORD: But look at me. Living on a stretcher like some war casualty. Dressing out of a suitcase. Flogging away at my desk. There's little enough to offer you.

ROSIE: Those things don't matter. It's the depths of you I'm interested in.

[TRAFFORD *thrusts.*]

Ooh. A little more to the right.

ASSESSOR: A little more to the right and we come upon the asbestos fireproof curtain. Mmm. Not of the highest quality. I shall make a note of that.

TRAFFORD: Oh. Contact! I think I'm taking off.

ROSIE: I'm with you.

ASSESSOR: Her Majesty's. Grand old theatre. Just down the street it was. Famous case. Considered by experts an exemplar of public safety. Fireproof seats. Fireproof floors and appliances. Fireproof paint. Fourteen tanks in the roof; fire-cocks with hose and nozzles on every floor and in all passages. Every possible precaution taken; every security adopted. Burned to the ground on Sunday morning, March twenty-third, 1902.

[TRAFFORD *and* ROSIE *thrash.*]

TRAFFORD: Uh . . . uh . . . uh . . .

ASSESSOR: In the Anthony Hordern's fire of 1901 an employee of the company, Harry Clegg, hounded by the flames, was forced to the roof of the six storey building. He stood there, intermittently visible through the rising clouds of smoke, watched by a crowd of thousands in the street below. With the hungry flames advancing, unable to be helped, having no way down . . . he stood erect, saluted the crowd before him, then jumped a hundred and twenty feet to his death splattered on the roadway below.

TRAFFORD: Aaaaargh!

ROSIE: Aaargh! Aaaargh! Aaaargh!

[ROSIE *and* TRAFFORD *stop thrashing.*]

ASSESSOR: A ladder had been fetched . . . the tallest in Sydney. It had failed to reach him by thirty feet.

TRAFFORD: Are you all right?

ROSIE: I think so. What about you?

[ROSIE *and* TRAFFORD *lie back.*]

ASSESSOR: A cameraman braving the intense heat of the conflagration captured the whole exciting and tragic incident on moving film.

[ROSIE *lights a cigarette with red-gloved hand and exhales.*]

ROSIE: It's a mad idea, isn't it?

TRAFFORD: I don't think so.

ASSESSOR: [*sniffing*] Smoke?

ROSIE: Burning down a theatre?

TRAFFORD: In my circumstances, it makes sense.

ASSESSOR: [*sniffing*] It *is* smoke.

ROSIE: Are you pleased I thought of it?

TRAFFORD: I think you're brilliant.

ROSIE: I only want us to be happy.

[*She passes the cigarette to him with her red-gloved hand.*]

ASSESSOR: [*still sniffing*] I'd better investigate.

[*Blackout.*]

SCENE FOUR

The stage. The INVESTIGATOR *sits in* TRAFFORD*'s chair with his feet on* TRAFFORD*'s desk. He cleans his fingernails with* TRAFFORD*'s pen.* TRAFFORD *and the* SOLICITOR *stand.*

TRAFFORD: Everything. I want to know everything she's doing.

INVESTIGATOR: Could be expensive.

SOLICITOR: What sort of information, precisely?

TRAFFORD: You might start with her fire-lighting activities, for example.

INVESTIGATOR: Arsin' around, is she?

SOLICITOR: Don't be cheap, Splatt. Arson has nothing to do with matrimonial investigations. As your solicitor, Mr Trafford, I advise you to seek proof of any . . . er . . . adulterous behaviour.

TRAFFORD: Get that too. If she's seeing anyone, I want to know. It would strengthen my case, wouldn't it?

SOLICITOR: Your case is strong enough. It's a man's world, the law.

INVESTIGATOR: But there's always a problem with investigating adultery.

SOLICITOR: What problem?

INVESTIGATOR: To prove adultery there must be penetration. Attempted intercourse does not in law constitute adultery unless actual penetration is proved or must be inferred, but complete penetration is not essential.

TRAFFORD: What does that all mean?

INVESTIGATOR: [*lasciviously*] It means I need to get a good close look.

SOLICITOR: A fine point of law, Mr Trafford. Don't worry about it. Now, is that all you want?

TRAFFORD: I wouldn't mind knowing where my son is. I haven't seen him for days.

SOLICITOR: Do you visit him?

TRAFFORD: She's changed the locks.

I can't get into my own house.

SOLICITOR: She wouldn't take off with your son, would she?

TRAFFORD: Take off?

SOLICITOR: Kidnap him.

TRAFFORD: She's off the rails, John. She might do anything.

SOLICITOR: Well, that's enough to go on, isn't it, Splatt?

INVESTIGATOR: [*rising arrogantly*] I suppose so. See ya, Trafford.

[*He exits.*]

SOLICITOR: [*reassuringly*] He's a genius, George. Just leave him to me.

[*The* SOLICITOR *exits, following the* INVESTIGATOR. ESSON *enters.*]

TRAFFORD: Ah. Esson. Good chap. We need to talk. Have a seat.

[TRAFFORD *pours two glasses from a bottle of wine. He seems keen to ply* ESSON *with alcohol.*]

ESSON: You've reconsidered my play?

TRAFFORD: Reconsidered it? It's already in production, old man.

ESSON: It is?

TRAFFORD: Cheers, then.

ESSON: Yes, of course. Cheers . . . It's such a surprise.

TRAFFORD: Opening night Thursday.

ESSON: So soon?

TRAFFORD: No point in keeping a top play like that hidden away in the drawer. Refill?

[*He charges his own glass too.*]

ESSON: I must admit I had misgivings.

TRAFFORD: Nonsense. Such as?

ESSON: Well. I thought . . . a little too intelligent, maybe?

TRAFFORD: Rubbish. Oh . . . we've changed a few things here and there. Refill?

[*He charges his own glass too.*]

ESSON: But . . . it's a socialist play.

TRAFFORD: Socialism. Marxism. Workers' ideals. All part of life's rich fabric.

ESSON: I had no idea you were so tolerant.

TRAFFORD: The century marches on. We can't afford to stagnate in the theatre. Refill?

[*He charges his own glass too.* HIGGS *and the* INSURANCE ASSESSOR *enter the wings. The* ASSESSOR *carries a fold-up easel, board and pointer.*]

HIGGS: . . . None of those canvases have got fireproof paint.

ASSESSOR: Let me see.

[*He looks and sniffs.*]

ESSON: Well, George, I'd like to drink to your health. I believe you've done a courageous and honourable thing.

TRAFFORD: Oh, no.

ESSON: Yes. Courageous and honourable. You've set the true Australian drama on the road to national acceptance. To you, sir.

[*They drink.*]

HIGGS: The fire escape out the back's rusted. The props room's a tinderbox: there's a box full of coloured fire stored there!

ASSESSOR: You've been most helpful, Mr Higgs.

HIGGS: Thank you, sir.

[HIGGS *exits. The* ASSESSOR *moves centre stage.*]

TRAFFORD: Ah. The insurance assessor, is it?

ASSESSOR: That's correct. Madden of Perpetual Life and Fire.

[*They shake hands.*]

TRAFFORD: Pleased to meet you. This is Mr Esson, a most distinguished playwright.

[*They shake hands.*]

ASSESSOR: How do you do? [*Beginning to set up the easel*] I understand, Mr Trafford, that you wish to vary your policy with us.

TRAFFORD: Yes, I do.

[ESSON *pours himself more from the bottle.*]

ESSON: [*happily*] Insurance is the opiate of the bourgeoisie.

ASSESSOR: Ahem. I have a little demonstration here. Do you mind?

TRAFFORD: Not at all.

ESSON: [*happily*] Not at all.

[*The* ASSESSOR *has set up on the easel a large diagram of the cross-section of a theatre. The* ASSESSOR *indicates with a pointer.*]

ASSESSOR: This theatre, gentlemen, in cross section. Very like any other. Main doors. Auditorium. Stage. Hanging loft. Ventilator. Note the shape? Reminds you of something? A fireplace and chimney, is it not? There's nothing so like the homely hearth . . . on a grand scale . . . as the modern stage theatre. Your theatre, Mr Trafford, is the perfect shape for an open fireplace. And according to the principles of the open fireplace, if you put flammable fuel here . . . e.g. wooden props, gauzy scenery . . . then set off a spark . . . gunshot, fireworks . . . up she goes, a grate full of flames, a chimney full of smoke, a blast of withering heat to shrivel the front rows then quickly scorch the balcony and gallery. In other words, sitting in a theatre is like sitting with your feet and face in the fireplace waiting for someone to come along and strike a match!

ESSON: [*pouring the last of the wine into his glass; derogatorily*] What an imagination.

ASSESSOR: Facts, my friend. Theatre buildings are risky as hell. But we insure them all the time. Theatre managers are among our best clients. Of course, they pay for it.

TRAFFORD: I understand, Mr Madden. Bigger policy, bigger premium. But nothing's too expensive where public safety is concerned.

ASSESSOR: My thoughts precisely, Mr Trafford. So, if we're agreed, I'll get back to the office and draw up something straight away.

TRAFFORD: Excellent. I'll see you out.

[TRAFFORD *and the* ASSESSOR *exit.* ESSON *sits on. He drains the last of the wine from his glass.* HIGGS *enters conspiratorially and sits.*]

HIGGS: I'm a great admirer of your newspaper articles.

ESSON: Really? Thank you.

HIGGS: Never miss an issue of *The Socialist*. I like your poetry too.

ESSON: Few people say that.

HIGGS: Your writing speaks to everyone. It has justice as its muse.

ESSON: I think you're trying to flatter me.

HIGGS: Now, take this play of yours . . . *The Time Is . . .*

ESSON: . . . *Not Yet Ripe*.

HIGGS: A worthy socialist play.

ESSON: More anarchist, I think.

HIGGS: Not at all. It's about truth: our truth, and their dishonesty. I think — we all do, the stagehands — we think it's a very fine piece of work. [*Pause.*] We're sorry it can't go on.

ESSON: How's that?

HIGGS: It's a pity it couldn't have been some right-wing nonsense. Trafford's an old trickster. We just can't afford to buckle under this time.

ESSON: I don't think I understand.

HIGGS: We're . . . sacrificing your play. What better proof of our genuine commitment? Strike action beginning with the opening night of a great socialist play! It won't be held against us that we bent our political principles just for a mate.

ESSON: You're going on strike?

HIGGS: For higher wages.

ESSON: On my first night?

HIGGS: For better conditions.

ESSON: There's not much consolation in it for me.

HIGGS: You do support the workers, don't you?

ESSON: Yes. But this means everything to me. I've not had a play produced before.

HIGGS: And it means everything to us. To hit Trafford now. Hard. New play, opening night. It's perfect.

ESSON: Hit him too hard and he might break. I don't think his financial situation's all that hot.

HIGGS: Get away. You're talking like a capitalist.

ESSON: I'm talking like someone who writes for his bread and butter.

HIGGS: Your fight's our fight. Your play calls for workers to rise up. Well, here we are: rising up! Anyway . . . I don't want to hurt you, but . . . I think Trafford may have purposely chosen your play to try to out-manoeuvre us. But we won't cave in. We're committed to Thursday night, unless he meets our demands.

[*Pause.* ESSON *upturns the wine bottle to no avail.*]

ESSON: Mm. His interest *was* sudden.

HIGGS: Of course it was.

ESSON: So much for tolerance. [*Standing up*] I need another drink.

[ESSON *exits.* HIGGS *waits a moment, then begins riffling through the papers on* TRAFFORD's *desk and looking in the drawers.* ROSIE *enters behind him.*]

ROSIE: Looking for something?

[HIGGS *pauses. He realises who it is without looking. He continues riffling.*]

HIGGS: I'm looking for a document with which to nail your precious Mr Trafford. Anything will do. A love letter from you might be perfect.

[ROSIE *grabs him. She tries to drag him from the desk.* TRAFFORD *enters.*]

TRAFFORD: What's going on?

HIGGS: [*breaking free*] Oh, Jesus.

[*He exits.*]

TRAFFORD: What's happening?

ROSIE: He was going through your desk.

[*Pause.*]

TRAFFORD: It's quite an act we'll have to put on if we go ahead with it.

ROSIE: But we're in the acting business.

TRAFFORD: I hadn't forgotten.

[FIRST STAGEHAND *enters pushing a trolley. On the trolley is the large wooden crate marked 'Inflammable Goods'.*]

Hullo, what's this?

FIRST STAGEHAND: Mr Higgs' orders. He reckons this is unsafe in the props room. Where should I put it?

TRAFFORD: [*calculatingly*] Mm. Leave it here. And the trolley.

FIRST STAGEHAND: [*shrugging*] OK.

[FIRST STAGEHAND *exits. The crate is*

left there. It stands like a silent third person. ESSON *enters. The wine has worked further on him. He has a new bottle in one hand, which he waves.*]

ESSON: Ahhh. There you are. Listen to this. [*Declaiming with appropriate dramatic gesture*]

> Bring wine, a gushing horn of
>   wine . . .
> Huge flagons we will quaff,
>   wanton, carouse,
> But nothing lose save sorrow.

Just wrote it. Dedicated it to the barmaid who slipped me this bottle. Nothing like poetry to ease the pain of loss.

TRAFFORD: Here. Have a glass.

[ESSON *swigs pointedly from the bottle.*]

ROSIE: What is it you've lost?

ESSON: Nothing. Nothing.

[*Pause.*]

Just faith. Friends, maybe.

TRAFFORD: [*not looking at him*] I would have thought you were about to gain in those respects.

ESSON: Yes. One might suppose so.

TRAFFORD: [*cautiously*] What's the matter?

ESSON: Hoh. What playwright cares about the ruination of his first play's first night? Poh. It's nothing. Nothing. I don't care. Why should I care?

TRAFFORD: [*paling*] I don't think I—

[ESSON *suddenly raises his clenched fist and begins singing—strongly, drunkenly, bitterly—the words of Havelock Ellis to the tune 'Silver Moonlight Winds'. There are tears in his voice. He is trying to convince himself.*]

ESSON: [*marching on the spot*]

> Onward, brothers, march still
>   onward,
> Side by side and hand in hand.

[*He circles* ROSIE *and* TRAFFORD.]

> We are bound for man's true
>   kingdom,
> We are an increasing band.

[*As* ESSON *exits singing, the lights turn to red.* ROSIE *and* TRAFFORD *stand stunned. The music continues in the background. Pause.*]

TRAFFORD: Everything must go smoothly on opening night.

[*Blackout. The music and* ESSON'S *singing continues.*]

SCENE FIVE

Lit by a red light in the wings left, the ACTING TROUPE *and stagehands watch silently as* ESSON *drunkenly marches around, saluting with his fist.*

ESSON: [*singing bitterly and forcefully*]

> Though the way seems often
>   doubtful,
> Hard the toil which we endure,
> Though at times our courage
>   falters,
> Yet the promised land is sure . . .

[*He exits left. Blackout. The music fades to a ticking sound.*]

SCENE SIX

The vignettes in the sequence are separated by sharp blackouts, like frames in a film. Throughout the whole scene there is a ticking noise (as of a clock or time-bomb device) which gradually crescendoes. By the end of the scene it is very loud. For the vignette effect, localised spots should be used

*over different parts of the stage and
wings.*

VIGNETTE 1

[*There is a soft ticking sound.*
TRAFFORD *and the* INSURANCE
ASSESSOR *sign a contract.*]

TRAFFORD: There it is. My perfectly
innocent signature.

ASSESSOR: That's all settled, then. It's a
pleasure doing business with you.

[*Momentary blackout and silence.*]

VIGNETTE 2

[HIGGS *and* FIRST STAGEHAND *chat.*]

FIRST STAGEHAND: I've been thinking
about this strike, sorter thing. He's a
good bloke, Esson.

HIGGS: He's one of them, mate.

FIRST STAGEHAND: But he writes about
us.

HIGGS: Don't be fooled, mate. He's
interested in words, not workers.

[*Momentary blackout and silence.*]

VIGNETTE 3

[ESSON *and* TRAFFORD.]

TRAFFORD: Just calm down, Louis.

ESSON: I don't like it. It's not right.
Let me take it home and rewrite it.

TRAFFORD: Don't be silly. It goes on
tomorrow night.

ESSON: But it's—it's passé. It's five years
out of date already. It's a disaster.

TRAFFORD: I think it's coming together
very nicely.

ESSON: The rehearsals are so awkward.
The lines have no grace. Perhaps it's
all been done with too much of a
rush.

TRAFFORD: Listen, Louis. This is the
theatre. Everything's done in a rush.

[*Momentary blackout and silence.*]

VIGNETTE 4

[MOLLY *and the* SOLICITOR.]

MOLLY: But he's having me followed!

SOLICITOR: Don't worry. It's all under
control.

[*Momentary blackout and silence.*]

VIGNETTE 5

[HIGGS *and the* ACTING TROUPE.]

HIGGS: We've got to show a united
front. You'll be blacklegging if you
don't join us.

OLD ACTOR: We're not scabs.

HIGGS: Prove it.

OLD ACTRESS: It's not our fight.

HIGGS: Still in love with starvation, are
we, dear?

[*Momentary blackout and silence.*]

VIGNETTE 6

[TRAFFORD *and* HIGGS.]

TRAFFORD: Be intelligent, Higgs. Call
this strike off. You're only working
against your own cause.

HIGGS: No we're not.

[*Momentary blackout and silence.*]

VIGNETTE 7

[FIRST STAGEHAND *is parking the
inflammable goods crate on the
trolley.* TRAFFORD *directs.*]

FIRST STAGEHAND: Right here?

TRAFFORD: It's only temporary.

FIRST STAGEHAND: [*shrugging*] Okay.

[*He starts tipping up crate.
Momentary blackout and silence.*]

VIGNETTE 8

[HIGGS *and* ROSIE.]

HIGGS: What are you and Trafford
up to?

ROSIE: Just leave me alone.

HIGGS: Don't think you'll outsmart
me, girl.

[*Momentary blackout and silence.*]

VIGNETTE 9

[ROSIE *and the* CARETAKER WOMAN. *The* CARETAKER WOMAN *scrubs. Her bird hangs in its cage nearby.*]

ROSIE: Let me have him at my place for a while.

CARETAKER WOMAN: Oh, no. I couldn't do that.

ROSIE: For a little holiday.

CARETAKER WOMAN: But he'd miss his mother.

[*Momentary blackout and silence.*]

VIGNETTE 10

[MOLLY *and the* SOLICITOR.]

MOLLY: [*holding a red glove*] He's got the other one. Don't you see what that means?

SOLICITOR: Why didn't you tell me this before?

[*Momentary blackout and silence.*]

VIGNETTE 11

[ROSIE *and* TRAFFORD. *By now the ticking noise is extremely loud.*]

TRAFFORD: There'll be a panic, but the new exits are there. No one'll be hurt.

ROSIE: I always imagined we'd do it late at night. With the place empty.

TRAFFORD: And create suspicion? No. To beat those insurance fellows you have to look them directly in the eye.

[*Blackout. Silence. Then the sudden, very loud, urgent ringing of an electric bell.*]

SCENE SEVEN

The wings. Opening night. The ACTING TROUPE *is dressed for* ESSON'S *play* The Time Is Not Yet Ripe. HIGGS *and the* STAGEHANDS *stand together threateningly.* ESSON *stands nervously holding a glass and a wine bottle, drinking.* ROSIE *is at* TRAFFORD'S *side.*

TRAFFORD: Ladies and gentlemen. Allow me to say, before we make a start, good luck to all of you. There's a fine tradition of drama on these boards. Mr Esson is a fine writer. No nerves now. Do your best. Curtain, Joe!

[*Blackout.*]

SCENE EIGHT

The painted backdrop for Act One of Esson's The Time Is Not Yet Ripe *depicts the Prime Minister's drawing-room.* TRAFFORD *and* ROSIE, *as Barrett and Doris, embrace. Their acting is melodramatic.*

ROSIE: [*with her head on* TRAFFORD'S *shoulder*] O, Sydney, this is all I want. No more. [*Pushing him away*] Sit down. Now! [*Taking a seat*] Do you admire me immensely?

[HIGGS *and the* STAGEHANDS *enter.*]

TRAFFORD: I do. You are quite perfect. But Doris . . .

ROSIE: But what?

HIGGS: Just a minute, Mr Trafford.

TRAFFORD: [*ignoring him*] You must give up your fashionable frivolity—

HIGGS: We're taking strike action, Mr Trafford.

[TRAFFORD *and* ROSIE *persist with the play.* TRAFFORD *rises and moves to the window, taking out a cigarette.*]

TRAFFORD: You are pursuing an illusory existence. It must end. Socialism demands it.

[*He lights the cigarette.*]

ROSIE: Is this a proposal?

HIGGS: [*advancing right across stage towards* TRAFFORD] We are in earnest, Mr Trafford.

[ESSON *enters drunkenly. He moves towards* HIGGS *with the wine bottle upraised.* STAGEHANDS *grab* ESSON.]

ESSON: Get off, you bastards!

TRAFFORD: Yes. I propose a revolution!

[TRAFFORD *flicks the lighted cigarette through the window. There is a violent explosion. Coloured fire streams into the set through the window, right into the faces of* TRAFFORD *and the* STAGEHANDS. TRAFFORD *is thrown backwards. The* STAGEHANDS *are in complete disarray. The* TROUPE *runs on. There are cries of 'Fire!' 'Get the asbestos curtain down!' 'Open the doors!' Pandemonium. Fire. Smoke. Bells ring. Panicking people run through. A great sound of fire spreading, etc.*]

SCENE NINE

During the fire. A drunken ESSON *wanders through in an anarchistic suicidal state. He touches something hot and laughs.* HIGGS *enters, tosses water from a bucket, exits.* ROSIE *and* TRAFFORD *enter.*

ESSON: [*fanning the flames*] Advance. Spread out. Take every theatre. Take the city. Take the suburbs. They're waiting for you.

TRAFFORD: How the conflagration spread! Nothing could have exceeded the rapidity with which the flames stampeded through the building.

ROSIE: I can't find the bird.

TRAFFORD: The flimsy scenery, the acres of canvas, the light construction of the robing rooms hung with gossamer costumes, the flooring, the curtains . . .

ROSIE: The cage door was open. The bird wasn't there.

ESSON: They're waiting for you. Newspapers, books, manuscripts, letters. Go on. The news-stands. The book-stalls. The libraries. Keep going. The shelves in every hideous lounge room in every appalling Australian home. They're waiting. They're trembling.

[HIGGS *re-enters. He tosses water from a bucket. He gives* ROSIE, TRAFFORD *and* ESSON *empty buckets. He exits.*]

TRAFFORD: The destruction of the stage was the work of minutes.

ROSIE: Oh, God, I hope he's flown away. Or someone's rescued him.

ESSON: Yes. Lick up the trouser leg of the worker reading his evening newspaper. Explode it in his hands. Jump across to where the housewife pores over a women's journal. Shrivel it to ashes. Rage along the lines of printer's ink. Leap into the eyes of the people!

[HIGGS *re-enters behind them. He is amazed to find them still standing where they were. He tosses his bucketful violently.*]

HIGGS: [*screaming*] Get water!

[*He exits.*]

TRAFFORD: The Empire's last act was a performance supreme in its scenic splendour. One of my best productions.

ESSON: Damn writing! If only words could *burn*.

[ESSON *wanders out.*]

ROSIE: Pretty Boy! Pretty Boy!

[ROSIE *exits, searching.* HIGGS *crosses. He notices and picks up a piece of burning wood, taking it with him as he exits.*]

TRAFFORD: [*unperturbed, pleased with himself*] From the stage the flames swept through the auditorium. And in the hotel next door, the beer boiled.

[*He exits.*]

[*Blackout.*]

SCENE TEN

The ruined stage. ROSIE, ESSON, *the* INSURANCE ASSESSOR, REPORTER *and a* POLICEMAN *all sift through or kick over the debris with varying degrees of commitment.* TRAFFORD, *by contrast, stands, head bowed, over a small pile of debris in front of him.*

ASSESSOR: Careful. Careful. Tread lightly. Every speck of ash tells a story.

REPORTER: [*taking notes*] Almost a major catastrophe. But thanks to new fire exits the public was evacuated without casualty.

ROSIE: [*bending down*] One little casualty.

ESSON: The path to glory is strewn with casualties.

ROSIE: [*picking up something small and charred*] Poor little Pretty Boy. Out of the birdcage into the fire.

ESSON: A brief moment of triumph. Then *fsst.*

ASSESSOR: Put it on the pile over there. It's evidence.

[*They all gather round the small pile with the exception of the* ASSESSOR *who keeps sifting. They take off their* hats. TRAFFORD *stands at the head of the group.*]

TRAFFORD: Dearly beloved, we are gathered here to lament the passing of the past.

ESSON: Here lies the charred little corpse of the Australian drama. Stillborn, in these ashes.

TRAFFORD: The Muses are in mourning. Comedy herself sheds a tear.

ROSIE: I still wish I could have saved him. I have a soft spot for birds.

TRAFFORD: She was a great old theatre, the Empire.

REPORTER: But there was new competition on the streets. She wasn't pulling them in like she used to.

ESSON: How long will it be before an Australian messianic drama stalks the stages, a scourge to Mammon and the Philistines?

TRAFFORD: She liked a nobbler and a good belly laugh. She's laid low now, the old Empire.

[*Bringing out a red glove suitably singed from his pocket and dropping it surreptitiously onto the pile.*]

A tragedy of our times.

ASSESSOR: [*coming across to them*] All right, then. I believe I have as much as I need.

[*With a trowel the* ASSESSOR *scoops up the pile of ashes (including the red glove) around which they have been standing. He tips it into a gleaming leather briefcase.*]

Back to the office to make my report.

[*Briefcase in hand, the* ASSESSOR *exits left. The others exit right as mourners from a funeral. In the wings* HIGGS *hands a charred piece of wood to the* ASSESSOR. *They exit together in conversation. Blackout.*]

SCENE ELEVEN

The ruined stage. ROSIE *and* TRAFFORD *enter, carrying picnic things.*

TRAFFORD: Where will our picnic be?

ROSIE: Right here. Watson's Bay.

TRAFFORD: Of course.

> [*He throws down a rug. She sits and opens a picnic basket. He looks at the wreckage behind.*]

If only I could lower a backdrop. A deserted beach scene.

ROSIE: We'll imagine it.

> [TRAFFORD *sits.*]

TRAFFORD: Mm. French bread.

ROSIE: And oysters.

TRAFFORD: Just like . . .

ROSIE: Of course.

> [*He picks up a bottle of wine to open it. He pauses, watching her set the things out.*]

TRAFFORD: Take your clothes off.

ROSIE: [*laughing*] I beg your pardon.

TRAFFORD: There's no one around. This beach is deserted, didn't you say? Take them off.

> [*Pause.*]

ROSIE: [*smiling*] OK.

> [*She takes her blouse off. He sits transfixed, looking at her, the wine bottle partly uncorked in his lap.*]

TRAFFORD: You're an inspiration. I look at you and something catches fire in me.

> [*He laughs.*]

Internal combustion. You fuel the motor of my soul.

> [*Pause.*]

We will fly, you know. Without wires. With film we'll take the man in the street into the air. We'll sell him a ticket to cloudland. The whole theatre will take off and soar across the city. We'll put wind in the audience's hair. We'll snatch the breath from their lungs. In wonder they'll look down on the suburbs, the sea, the paddocks; they'll see themselves vanishing to faraway dots . . .

> [MOLLY *enters.*]

MOLLY: Well, well. What a cosy little scene.

> [ROSIE *covers herself.*]

TRAFFORD: What a sense of timing.

MOLLY: It always was my forte.

TRAFFORD: [*indicating the ruins*] Not much use to you now, though.

MOLLY: Only a person totally devoid of feeling could do this.

TRAFFORD: Is that how you describe yourself, Mrs Red Glove?

> [*Ignoring him, she looks around.*]

MOLLY: It's like coming back to your childhood home and finding it gone. It empties you. Perhaps that's a good thing. It's easier to be honest when you're empty.

TRAFFORD: So you're going to confess?

MOLLY: I'm going to America.

TRAFFORD: What?

MOLLY: I'm going to have a new career. New York, I fancy. Or Hollywood. Have you heard of Hollywood? A few sandy streets and a patch of scrub, they say. But the rumour is: it's going to be big. And close to the Mexican border. Ideal for quick divorces.

TRAFFORD: I'm tempted to bid you good riddance. But there's the small matter of arson which I'm sure the police will be keen to see you about. Once the assessor has made his report.

MOLLY: You'll not stop me, George.

I'll be on the next ship that leaves port.

TRAFFORD: There's no point trying, my dear. I have a private investigator tailing you. He'll inform the police as soon as you attempt to abscond.

MOLLY: Oh, yes. The private investigator. Watching my every move, isn't he? I just love an audience. [*Beginning to exit*] Oh, and by the way. My solicitor informs me that half the insurance money will be mine. It's the law. So I'll be well off in Hollywood, won't I?

[*She exits.*]

TRAFFORD: [*rising and shouting after her*] Don't be so sure of that. It's a man's world, the law.

ROSIE: [*beginning to pack the things away*] I don't think this picnic was such a good idea.

[*Enter* HIGGS.]

HIGGS: Well, well. Waiting for the insurance assessor's report, are we? I wonder what he's assessing right now.

TRAFFORD: Is your memory not so good, Higgs?

HIGGS: [*to* ROSIE] Now that the great Mr Trafford — the King of Melodrama — is ruined —

TRAFFORD: I am not ruined.

HIGGS: I see.

TRAFFORD: I shall rebuild.

HIGGS: With what?

TRAFFORD: The insurance money.

HIGGS: Oh, yes. The insurance money. If you get it.

TRAFFORD: Your memory is certainly failing. Shall I refresh it? You and your henchman are sadly out of a job. Being thus unemployed, you should be down at the pub enjoying yourselves.

HIGGS: Don't worry, Mr Trafford. I'm enjoying myself. Seeing the place in ruins. Thinking about boxes of inflammable goods.

TRAFFORD: Oh, dear. Is that what you're thinking about? Hadn't you better watch your step, Mr Higgs? The incendiarist tendencies of unionists are well known. I wouldn't like to have to mention *your* name to the police in connection with arson.

HIGGS: I doubt you would dare do that, sir.

TRAFFORD: I would if you forced me. I don't see that it presents a scenario difficult to follow: not satisfied that the effects of your strike would ruin me sufficiently, you sought to defeat and humiliate me completely by burning down my theatre. It's such a horrible concept, I can hardly bear to think about it. Yet — woolsheds were burnt down by striking shearers. Why not theatres by striking stagehands? But I would prefer to be kind: to rebuild and forget about it. I hope you see the point.

HIGGS: I see the point more clearly than ever. Luckily I've already covered myself. The insurance assessor has the full story about the box of inflammable goods. I expect justice will prevail.

[HIGGS *exits.* TRAFFORD *starts after him, but stops. He vents his rage by violently kicking a piece of debris. He hurts his toe.*]

TRAFFORD: Jesus Christ. [*Seeing* ROSIE *packing away the last of the picnic things*] Hey. What about our picnic?

ROSIE: It's turned sour.

TRAFFORD: You've not gone crook on me, have you?

ROSIE: I'm depressed by all this

wreckage. Things have turned out so ugly.

TRAFFORD: It *has* become complicated. But we'll act it out. We're in the profession, remember?

ROSIE: I don't want to *act* it out. George. Look what we've done. We've lied, we've cheated. We've endangered people's lives. We've become criminals.

TRAFFORD: For the sake of something good.

ROSIE: But see what we've got. Is this what the vision was supposed to look like?

TRAFFORD: We'll rebuild. You said you'd joined me.

ROSIE: I tried to. I tried to join you, deep down.

TRAFFORD: Exploring my interior?

ROSIE: I seem to have discovered more than I bargained for. About myself too.
[*Pause.*]
I think we've made a big mistake.

TRAFFORD: *We've* made a mistake? This was your idea, don't forget. Don't blame me for this charred mess. You were the one who came up with the idea of a fire.

ROSIE: But I got it from inside you.

TRAFFORD: Listen. The red glove fits you too. Perfect fit, didn't you say?
[ROSIE *grabs up the picnic basket and rug.*]

ROSIE: Blame whoever you like. Just don't blame yourself, will you?
[*She exits. He goes after her.*]

TRAFFORD: [*pleading*] Rosie.
[*He stops. She has gone. He comes back. He looks defeated.*]
[*Imagining he hears a sound*] Rosie? Mr Madden?

[*There is no one there. From his pocket he takes a strip of film. He stands to hold it to the light. He declaims, actor-like.*]
Is life a moving picture? Each day a little square of light separated from the others by a strip of darkness? And Time, the Great Projectionist, rolling us on? Roll me on then, sir! Give my plot that comic twist! Take that old reel out and burn it, sir! Take that old reel out and burn it . . .
[*The lights fade. Blackout. The sound of an old fashioned projector whirring up. A piano begins to play.*]

The vignettes in this sequence include and are separated by sharp blackouts. During blackouts a slide showing written dialogue, etc, may appear large on a screen at the back. Piano music accompanies the action. The whole sequence is designed to reproduce the effect of a silent movie. It is all in black and white. Movements are jerky and melodramatic. Characters' lips move, but no sound issues. Light is flickery.

VIGNETTE 1

SLIDE: After the Disaster
[HIGGS *and* ROSIE *amongst the debris.* ROSIE *is tragically dejected.* HIGGS *comes by and is sympathetic.*]

SLIDE: 'You poor woman. May I help in any way?'
[TRAFFORD *becomes obvious in the wings spying on them.* ROSIE *demonstrates raptures of gratefulness to* HIGGS.]

SLIDE: 'You are too kind, Mr Higgs.'
[HIGGS *sidles up to whisper in* ROSIE's *ear. Much eye-rolling, etc.* TRAFFORD *cups his ear, trying to hear.*]

SLIDE: 'What is it you see in that old fool, Trafford?'

[ROSIE *turns and smiles at* HIGGS.]

SLIDE: 'Nothing now, I assure you, Mr Higgs.'

[HIGGS *and* ROSIE *exit arm in arm.* TRAFFORD *rages. Blackout.*]

VIGNETTE 2

SLIDE: Later

[HIGGS *and* TRAFFORD *amongst the debris.* ROSIE *watches in alarm, hands to head, etc.* TRAFFORD *has* HIGGS *by the lapels. He shakes him fiercely.* HIGGS *drops suddenly to his knees.* TRAFFORD *shakes him some more.*]

SLIDE: 'Leave, Mr Higgs. You're trespassing.'

[HIGGS *waves his arms and tries to push* TRAFFORD *off.*]

SLIDE: 'You're wrong, Trafford. There's no trespassing for those in search of justice. Admit it. You're a criminal!'

[*Enraged,* TRAFFORD *punches* HIGGS *in the face.* HIGGS *talks on.*]

SLIDE: 'Hit me all you like. I speak as your conscience.'

[TRAFFORD *punches* HIGGS *again.* HIGGS *falls over backwards.* TRAFFORD *goes to kick* HIGGS. ROSIE *intervenes.*]

SLIDE: 'Stop! Stop! You're acting like little boys.'

[HIGGS *gets up, picks up his hat and exits.* ROSIE *clings to* TRAFFORD *who gesticulates wildly.*]

SLIDE: 'What are you protecting him for?'

[ROSIE *clings tighter.*]

SLIDE: 'It wasn't him I was protecting.'

[TRAFFORD *rages as she clings to him. Blackout.*]

VIGNETTE 3

SLIDE: Later Still

[TRAFFORD *amongst the debris. The*

INSURANCE ASSESSOR *arrives.*]

SLIDE: The Insurance Assessor

[TRAFFORD *and the* ASSESSOR *shake hands.* TRAFFORD *is nervous. The* ASSESSOR *takes an immensely thick report from his briefcase.*]

SLIDE: The Report!

[*The* ASSESSOR *hands the report to* TRAFFORD. TRAFFORD *reads it ravenously.*]

SLIDE: What Does It Say?

[TRAFFORD *gets to the end of the thick report in record time. A big smile breaks over his face.*]

SLIDE: The Report is Favourable!

[TRAFFORD *and the* ASSESSOR *shake hands warmly.* TRAFFORD *slaps him on the back, brings out some cigars. They light up with much back-slapping, hand-shaking and gesticulation. Blackout.*]

VIGNETTE 4

SLIDE: Even Later

[ROSIE *amongst the debris.* TRAFFORD *enters. She flees, but he catches her. She is fearful. He embraces her. He speaks.*]

SLIDE: He Tells Her The News

[*They embrace comprehensively. She drops to her knees with relief. He gesticulates.*]

SLIDE: 'We did it! We have the money!'

[*More embracing. She gesticulates and clutches his legs.*]

SLIDE: Dreams Can Come True!

[*He lifts her to her feet. They dance together, wildly waltzing in the ruins.*]

SLIDE: But . . . What's This?

[HIGGS *enters surreptitiously while they continue dancing. His eyes are darkened, he looks fiendish. He bends*

*down and picks up items from the
debris.*]

SLIDE: *A static close-up of a woman's
glove and a piece of wood. On the
wood is written 'Inflammable Goods'.*

[HIGGS *waves the items triumphantly.
He begins to exit.* TRAFFORD *and*
ROSIE *suddenly stop dancing.*
TRAFFORD *shields* ROSIE *behind him
with his outstretched left arm and
with a gun in his outstretched right
hand shoots* HIGGS. HIGGS *falls flat on
his back and is motionless.* ROSIE *and*
TRAFFORD *stare at the corpse in
horror. Blackout. The projector
sound winds down. So too the piano.*

The lights come up on TRAFFORD *still
looking at the strip of film.* ESSON
and the CARETAKER WOMAN *have
entered behind him. They are arm in
arm, somewhat wobbly. She carries a
blackened birdcage.*]

ESSON: [*singing* The Wedding March]
Dah-dah-de-dah. Dah-dah-de-dah.

TRAFFORD: [*startled and disoriented by
his daydream*] Oh . . . Esson . . . Er,
Mrs Wailes.

ESSON: Congratulate us, George!

TRAFFORD: Good heavens. What for!

CARETAKER WOMAN: [*disengaging her
arm*] Give it a breeze, mate!

[*The* CARETAKER WOMAN *takes a
wine bottle from* ESSON'*s coat pocket.
She swigs roughly from it.*]

ESSON: Isn't she a vision? You never
told me you were hiding this genuine
original, George.

[*The* CARETAKER WOMAN *accidentally
drops the bottle.* ESSON *retrieves it
hurriedly.*]

TRAFFORD: Are you all right, Mrs
Wailes?

CARETAKER WOMAN: Oh. I'm boshter,
Mr Trafford. I'm on me way now,
ain't I? I'm in that lane with no
turning.

TRAFFORD: Pardon?

CARETAKER WOMAN: Through the
Domain to the morgue. The vagrant's
progress, they call it.

TRAFFORD: I'm terribly sorry.

CARETAKER WOMAN: I did have a bit
put away, you know. For a rainy day.
Safe as a bank I thought it was, my
little nest egg. [*Indicating the
blackened birdcage*] Had it hid under
the tray here. [*Shaking ash from the
cage*] Ashes now. Life's a snag, ain't
it?

ESSON: God, George. How's the heart
and soul, eh? Isn't she the future
hope of the Australian stage, our
Fanny?

CARETAKER WOMAN: I don't want to be
a bloomin' actress.

ESSON: A lump of uncrushed ore!

CARETAKER WOMAN: I'm a caretaker.
Caretakin's me profession, more's the
pity.

ESSON: A symbol of everything the
Australian drama is running away
from! But I shall lead the way back to
you, my dear.

[*He pinches her cheek. She brushes
his hand away.*]

I shall announce the banns! Drama
and reality!

TRAFFORD: What are you prattling
about, Louis?

ESSON: Real stuff! People! The way
they talk and move. The kitchen sink.
The workshop. The gutter. Real
theatre!

CARETAKER WOMAN: Sounds more like
real life. Who needs it?

TRAFFORD: No such thing as documentary theatre, Louis. Aren't you talking about the cinematographe?

ESSON: Aaaargh. Don't say that word.

TRAFFORD: Bioscope? Vitascope?

ESSON: Aaaargh. Just as bad.

TRAFFORD: They're the eyes of the twentieth century, I'm told.

ESSON: Pluck them out, then. I know what you're doing here. You want to rebuild the theatre as a moving picture palace, don't you?

TRAFFORD: That was the idea.

ESSON: So I've brought along this piece of real life to remind you of your folly.

TRAFFORD: My folly was in too long burying myself beneath the burden of live theatre. Carrying that damned living world up the stage ramp night after night. Only to see it roll back down every curtain. Shakespeare's Globe! Hah! The *torment* of keeping disbelief suspended!

ESSON: But, George. Your cinematographe won't sweat. It won't threaten to spill into the audience. Neither fat nor full, 'tis flat and mean. Your cinematographe is as dull and two-dimensional as the commercial narrow-mindedness from whose sordid loins it sprang—

CARETAKER WOMAN: Chain it up, Lou. I thought you said you'd find me a job.

ESSON: [*continuing to address* TRAFFORD, *but holding the* CARE-TAKER WOMAN'*s sleeve to prevent her leaving*] The theatre's an old scrubber, I accept. But hasn't she got guts? And generosity. Her proscenium welcomes with open arms. Your new tarted-up cinema? Brassy, cold, mechanical. No human contact . . .

[*The* CARETAKER WOMAN *taps him on the head.*]

Eh?

CARETAKER WOMAN: [*with a hard edge to her voice*] Dibs, Lou. Darbies, remember? Bees and honey . . .

ESSON: What?

CARETAKER WOMAN: Money! You said that's what we were coming here for.

ESSON: Er, yes.

TRAFFORD: I'm skint, Louis. I can't offer any compensation.

ESSON: No, no. I was thinking Fanny could do a little job for us. To help her out. But I'm sure she won't mind putting the first session on the slate, will you, luv?

CARETAKER WOMAN: [*concealing her mounting anger*] What is it I'm supposed to do?

ESSON: Well, I was thinking you might model for us.

CARETAKER WOMAN: [*drawing her coat around her*] Eh? What do you think I am?

ESSON: No, no. Just talk. Let George hear your voice. And . . . and move around a bit. [*To* TRAFFORD] She's a walking social document. Real life! It's marvellous.

[*The* CARETAKER WOMAN *walks, then turns and puts down birdcage. She puts her hands on her hips.*]

CARETAKER WOMAN: Well, gents. I'm not a hintellectual. But I've cottoned onto what you're spruikin' about. And basically I think you're full of shit.

ESSON:
TRAFFORD: } Eh?

CARETAKER WOMAN: You men! Pretending you're so concerned. The theatre this—real life that. Blow the froth off, will you! I'm sick of men and their flash talk, their brave promises. Big minds they reckon they've got, big hearts. Big heads is what. And I'm sick of cleaning up after them. 'Caretaker Woman'. I've been one all me life. Because men don't know how to take care of anything. Not even themselves. If it wasn't for the caretakers—us women—men'd be up to their ears in the dung-heap of their own mess: empty bottles! stained laundry! bloody bandages! [*Looking around*] Of course, there are some messes too big even for a woman . . . Call me if you want any more modelling done. Good day, gents.

[*She picks up the birdcage and exits.* TRAFFORD *and* ESSON *are left gaping.*]

ESSON: Good God. What a bitch!

TRAFFORD: [*depressed*] Didn't leave us much, did she?

ESSON: Who would have thought the average woman harboured such resentments?

TRAFFORD: When women tell the truth there's never much in it for men.

ESSON: Eh?

[*Realising* TRAFFORD *has been hard hit. He sits* TRAFFORD *down on a charred piece of debris.*]

Hey. Come on, old fella.

TRAFFORD: Women keep us up, don't they? Us and our illusions. I wish Rosie was here.

ESSON: Listen. What you need is a good stiff drink. I'll just pop down to the bar. Don't do anything silly, now.

[ESSON *exits. Enter the* INSURANCE ASSESSOR *and* HIGGS.]

ASSESSOR: Awfully sorry to interrupt, Mr Trafford. Could I see you in private?

TRAFFORD: Here is as private as we'll get, Mr Madden.

ASSESSOR: [*fishing in his briefcase*] Very well. It's nothing, really. I'm sure it can all be explained.

[*He pulls out the red glove and the charred piece of wood which reads 'Inflammable Goods'. They have official-looking identification tags attached. He hands them to* TRAFFORD.]

Have you seen either of these items before?

TRAFFORD: [*very subdued*] This is a woman's glove. This is a piece from a box of chemicals we had here.

ASSESSOR: Could either of these have had anything to do with starting the fire?

HIGGS: Tell the truth, Trafford.

TRAFFORD: I suppose they could have.

ASSESSOR: Mr Higgs here says you had that box specially placed behind the set just prior to the opening night's performance.

HIGGS: Admit it, Trafford.

TRAFFORD: Mr Higgs is . . . [*faltering as something inside him collapses. Very softly*] Mr Higgs is telling the truth.

[*Pause.*]

ASSESSOR: Well. It's out of my hands now.

[*He takes the glove and the piece of wood from* TRAFFORD *and puts them back into the briefcase.*]

I'm afraid it's a matter for the police. Justice will prevail, I'm sure. Good day to you.

[*The* ASSESSOR *exits.* TRAFFORD *doubles up and falls sideways from where he sits.* ESSON, *carrying a bottle, enters to find* HIGGS *standing over the fallen* TRAFFORD. *Blackout.*]

SCENE TWELVE

The ruined stage, a while later. ESSON,
HIGGS *and* TRAFFORD *sit in a circle on
pieces of debris. Several empty bottles
litter the ground. They have done a lot
of drinking.* TRAFFORD *faces the
audience. He is extremely pale, and
appears to be propped up. He has on
an aviator's cap and goggles.* HIGGS *has
fashioned a paper plane. He shows it
off.* HIGGS *and* ESSON *laugh madly.*
ESSON *grabs the plane, and goes to
throw it.* HIGGS *and* ESSON *laugh madly.*
TRAFFORD *grabs it.*

TRAFFORD: All I wanted was to say
something.

[*The others laugh madly.*]

To show something.

[*More mad laughter.*]

Something deep, important. Anything
would have done — so long as it
proved me . . . capable.

[*More mad laughter.* TRAFFORD
laughs with them. HIGGS *strikes a
match and sets fire to the tail of the
plane. Great laughter.* TRAFFORD
*throws the plane. They all laugh as
the burning plane falls. The sound of
an aeroplane passes thunderously
loudly overhead. They all duck.*]

ESSON: Good God.

HIGGS: That was close.

TRAFFORD: I need another drink.

[*He pours one.*]

HIGGS: You're a real mate, Georgie. I
thought us stagehands were goners
there for a while. You could have
stuck it on us, you know. It was
bloody good of you to take the rap.

ESSON: My thoughts precisely. You're
a bloody gentlemen, George. And
we're with you. That's what we have
to do, us males. Stand together in the
face of adversity.

TRAFFORD: [*seriously*] What adversity?
Women? Truth? Ourselves?

ESSON: I was thinking of the law,
old man.

[ESSON *pours more wine. Enter the*
INVESTIGATOR.]

TRAFFORD: Oh. Splatt.

INVESTIGATOR: Thought I'd better
come round and tell you. Your wife
left the country this morning.

TRAFFORD: She did, eh?

INVESTIGATOR: On the *Wyoming*. She
took the child. Used the name of
Marsh.

TRAFFORD: Her old stage name.

INVESTIGATOR: *Mister* Marsh. She was
dressed as a man. She had the kid in
a tea-chest. That's how she gave me
the slip.

TRAFFORD: Perhaps her best
performance.

INVESTIGATOR: I thought he — I mean,
she — was one of the carrier's men. I
let him go. By the time I realised, the
ship had sailed. I engaged the police.
They boarded her off Watson's Bay.
They apprehended your wife, I mean
Mister Marsh, on the deck. It seems
he then suddenly removed his clothes
and the coppers fell back in disarray.
A wonderful weapon, nakedness — in
women. She came after them and
they retreated over the side of the
ship and fell down into their boat.
The *Wyoming* sailed on for America.

TRAFFORD: Quite a finale.

[*Enter the* SOLICITOR.]

SOLICITOR: Ah. There you are, George.

INVESTIGATOR: I was just telling Mr
Trafford about his wife's final
performance.

SOLICITOR: Ah, yes. She has escaped. Are you thinking of doing the same?

TRAFFORD: Leaving the country?

SOLICITOR: I have contacts. They could smuggle you away. But as your solicitor I must advise that such practices are outside the law.

TRAFFORD: [*shaking his head*] I shan't be taking any overseas trips.

SOLICITOR: Very well, then. The police are on their way here, I understand. They're also looking for a Miss Rosie Bellowes.

TRAFFORD: Oh, no. I hope she's got away.

SOLICITOR: So you'll be giving yourself up?

TRAFFORD: Yes. That's what I'll do. Give myself up.

SOLICITOR: Well, in case you crave a brief revenge along the way, may I suggest — as your solicitor, of course — that any blows you wish to land on members of the police force should be landed in the region of the groin. It's the only part of themselves they don't like making an exhibit of in court.

TRAFFORD: Thank you for the tip. I doubt I'll be needing it.

SOLICITOR: Well, that about wraps it up. I'll look forward to your instructions prior to the trial. Arson cases are my specialty. Some deliciously fine points of law. [*Shaking hands with* TRAFFORD] Good day, George.

INVESTIGATOR: I'll send my bill.

[*The* INVESTIGATOR *and* SOLICITOR *exit.* TRAFFORD *moves around a little, slowly. He looks about him.*]

TRAFFORD: The police are on their way . . .

HIGGS: First offence, mate. You'll be right.

ESSON: It's a world of gentlemen, the law. They understand a man's problems.

TRAFFORD: A world of men, eh?

HIGGS: They'll go easy. You confessed.

ESSON: They won't hang you.

TRAFFORD: [*ripping off the flying cap and goggles*] I'm leaving the world of men.

[TRAFFORD *rushes out. Blackout on* HIGGS *and* ESSON. *Spot on* TRAFFORD *in the wings.*]

'O for a muse of fire, that would ascend
The brightest heaven of invention:
A kingdom for a stage, princes to act,
And monarchs to behold the swelling scene!'

[*Pause.*]

'But pardon, gentles all,
The flat unraised spirits that hath dared
On this unworthy scaffold [*indicating self*] to bring forth . . .
So great . . . an . . . object . . .'

[*Pause. He goes blank. Blackout.*]

SCENE THIRTEEN

TRAFFORD *at the beach at night. He takes off his clothes. He piles them neatly. He walks into the sea. The sound of sea grows to a deafening pitch; then silence. Blackout.*

SCENE FOURTEEN

The ruined stage. Night. A POLICEMAN, *dimly lit, stands guard in the wings left.* ROSIE *enters right. She moves stealthily. She finds and picks up the flying cap and goggles. She throws them back down. The sound causes the* POLICEMAN *to turn, but he does not investigate. There is a sound off right.* ROSIE *hides.* TRAFFORD *enters. He is partly dressed but sopping wet.* ROSIE *steps out.*

ROSIE: George?

TRAFFORD: Rosie! You're back!

ROSIE: [*indicating the* POLICEMAN] Shhh!

TRAFFORD: I know. I confessed. They're after me.

ROSIE: And me.

[*Pause. She touches him.*]

You're all wet.

TRAFFORD: I've been swimming.

ROSIE: Putting out the fire?

TRAFFORD: Drowning. Diving. I don't know.

ROSIE: Suiciding, I expect you mean.

TRAFFORD: Didn't succeed at it. The waves spat me back again.

[*Pause.*]

I went all the way to the bottom, though. Totally black, it is, the sea floor at night. There's nothing at all. No sound, smell, sight. Just the feeling of the shape of yourself defined by black water.

[*Pause.*]

Why are you here?

ROSIE: To find out what's happening.

TRAFFORD: You'd be better off running for your life.

ROSIE: You can't just leave a country all of a sudden. Not when you've become part of it, fought for it.

TRAFFORD: Please go. It's me they want. I'm the criminal.

ROSIE: I can't go, George. There's no point in flight. Do you know, this afternoon I took a ride with that aviator fellow. I got him to pass low over here. I expect you may have seen us. I saw you — a blurred dot, you were. What I learned up there was the impossibility of exploration from the air. Sure, everything's laid out before you, but it's like trying to know a country from its map in an atlas. You can't do it. You've got to go in on foot, hack through the jungles, plumb the inland seas.

TRAFFORD: I know. Flying has to be done with your feet on the ground.

ROSIE: [*taking his hand*] Contact.

[*They look out at the audience. Gradually their voices rise to a shout.*]

TRAFFORD: We're moving?

ROSIE: You feel it?

TRAFFORD: A rumble underfoot.

ROSIE: An ancient turning.

TRAFFORD: We hurtle forward.

ROSIE: Horizon tilting!

TRAFFORD: The void upon us.

[*The* POLICEMAN *takes out some handcuffs and moves towards them.*]

ROSIE: We plummet!

TRAFFORD: We climb!

ROSIE: This world!

TRAFFORD: This speck!

[ROSIE *and* TRAFFORD *stand stock still, hand in hand, rooted to the stage, leaning forward, peering ahead. The* POLICEMAN *advances from behind. Blackout.*]

THE END

Patron of the arts
Sponsor of sport

**From West End musicals and ballet to tennis and cricket,
The Benson and Hedges Company is a major sponsor
of cultural and sporting activities in Australia.**

**The Company takes pride in knowing its wide support is
benefiting both participants and audiences alike.**

**The Benson and Hedges Company is proud to sponsor the
State Theatre Company of South Australia
in the Playhouse of the Adelaide Festival Centre in 1985.**

The
BENSON and HEDGES
Company

ARTISTIC DIRECTOR Keith Gallasch ASSOCIATE DIRECTOR Peter King GENERAL MANAGER Lyn Tuit FINANCE MANAGER Nigel Bray PRODUCTION MANAGER Grahame Murray DIRECTOR, MAGPIE Geoffrey Rush DEVELOPMENT MANAGER Josie Dowling SUBSCRIPTIONS MANAGER Beryl Lewis PUBLICITY MANAGER Lindsay Smith PUBLICITY ASSISTANT Robyn Seidel STAFF DESIGNER Ken Wilby ASSISTANT DESIGNER Colin Mitchell LIGHTING DESIGNER John Comeadow GRAPHIC DESIGNER Mark Thompson OFFICE MANAGER Mirella Innocente EXECUTIVE SECRETARY Sarah Jackson MAGPIE/PRODUCTION SECRETARY Nicki Sharrad SUBSCRIPTIONS ASSISTANT Joan Lucas RECEPTIONIST Candida Lucia-Brown RESOURCE OFFICER Rose Wilson STAGE MANAGERS Shauna Roche, Julie-Ann Willems, Steven Ford (Magpie) ASSISTANT STAGE MANAGERS Jenny Enilane, Linda Aitken PLAYHOUSE ENSEMBLE Natalie Bate, Terence Crawford, Peter Finlay, Douglas Hedge, David Kendall, Deborah Kennedy, Joan Murray, Dina Panozzo, Morna Seres, Andrew Tighe, Ross Williams, William Zappa MAGPIE ACTORS Louise Blackwell, Kristoffer Greaves, Evdokia Katahanas, Stephen Rae, Melanie Salomon WORKSHOP MANAGER Norm Callender MECHANISTS Rodney Ewell, Glen Finch, Keith Green, Steven Conroy PROPERTIES Graham Raven, Ross Howard, John Meyer HEAD SCENIC ARTIST Mac Dick SCENIC ARTIST Jane Corbel WARDROBE SUPERVISOR Bronwyn Jones COSTUME CUTTER Mari Galan COSTUME MAKERS Sue Nicola, Marione Mansfield TAILOR George Jukes MILLINER Helga Bechler BUYER Miriam Ready COSTUME SHOP HIRE MANAGER Yvonne Kuhn COSTUME HIRE ASSISTANTS Lillian Withers, Norma Lucas PROP SHOP MANAGER John Kuhn AFCT THEATRE MANAGER George Pullen HOUSE MANAGERS John Glennon, Douglas Dick CASUAL OFFICE ASSISTANT Bernadette Brzezinski BOARD OF GOVERNORS Malcolm Gray (Chairman), Jill Blewett, Maurice Crotti, Michael Harrison, Timothy Healy (Subscriber Representative), Rosemary Wighton (Subscriber Representative), Ken Wilby.

The State Theatre Company of South Australia is a founder member of the Confederation of Australian Professional Performing Arts Ltd.